Then Came The Baby

Then Came The Baby

The Wonder, Mayhem, and Hilarity of Our First Year as Parents

TIM AND OLIVE CHAN

ISBN: 0991810961
ISBN-13: 978-0-9918109-6-3

Cover design by Bill Vaxevanis
Cover and book illustrations by Olive Chan
Interior design and typesetting by Tim Chan

For Alena Joy Chan.

Contents

The Ride As Individuals   53

The Ride As a Couple   87

Introduction

"What's it like, being a new parent?" We would pause for a moment and begin to answer, and then our baby would spit up. Or cry. Or fart. Or do something amazingly cute like wave her fist and everyone would say, "Awww…" and promptly forget what we were talking about.

We were often relieved to evade such a difficult question. Life as a new parent involved so many feelings – how could we ever explain it in one sentence? It was wonderfully joyful and dreadfully awful at the same time. It was a roller coaster of emotions: euphoria, happiness, pride, wonder, and fascination, mixed in with exhaustion, frustration, anger, and anxiety.

This book is the story of our first year of parenting. It is our attempt of an answer to that hard-to-answer question. In it, we reflect on the experiences and changes that come with being a first-time mom and a first-time dad.

Similar to our first book, "Fight With Me: How We Learned to Be Married," this book is not a how-to book, but rather a how-we book. Every family is different; every child is different, as is every couple. Our experiences could be very similar to another family's – or it could be vastly different. Whatever the case, our hope is that our experiences might serve to encourage you, our reader.

Why did we write this book?

First, we wanted to give an honest and intimate picture of the secret life of new parents. Once a couple has a baby, they often disappear from the world. They stop going out and hide away in their caves. No one knows what their life is really like… until now.

This book compares and contrasts our perspectives as a new father and new mother and highlights how we can feel similarly or completely different about the same situation. It's also a window into how having a baby affected our marriage relationship.

Second, we wanted to give our child (and hopefully, children) an example of how to live life fully. We believe that is one of our primary responsibilities as parents. The best way to teach living life fully is to model it. Life is about learning to embrace the pleasant and difficult things, and having the courage to be vulnerable with ourselves and with others about what we feel and who we are.

Third, we wanted to show our child that she is loved and worthy of love, no matter how she feels and how her parents (or other people) feel. Emotions are part of what makes us human and knowing that we are unconditionally loved gives us freedom and courage to embrace the whole range of them. By being vulnerable about our experiences, we wanted to demonstrate that both positive and negative emotions are accepted in our family and that we are loved inclusive of how we feel.

Fourth, we wanted to share how being parents caused us

to change and grow. Parenthood was an invitation for us to mature as people. It was also an invitation to play and to remember the joy and simplicity of childhood.

This is our story of learning to love our child and the emotional roller coaster we experienced as parents, as individuals, as a couple and as part of a larger community of family and friends. We've structured our book by grouping the emotions in relation to these particular roles.

Emotional experiences are complex. For simplicity's sake, we have chosen to focus on one particular emotion at a time. But in reality, we felt more than one thing at any given point.

Who did we write this book for?

We wrote this book for people who are thinking about having children in the future, whether they are single or married. We wrote it for those who are curious about what it is like. It's our perspective, our real and personal experience.

We also wrote this book for parents with children, to share our experience and story in hopes that you will find something that resonates with you in your own parenting journey. We want to say to you, "You are not alone; others feel this way, too."

We wrote this for anyone who knows a new parent so that you can better empathize with the new parents in your life; to know better how to help them, love them and support them. We, as new parents, need you.

Lastly, we wrote this for Alena. We hope you will always remember how deeply loved you are, darling, even from the very beginning of your life.

Prologue

[Tim]

Theoretically, we were well prepared to be parents.

Both Olive and I are planners and we thrive on creating and executing plans. We like to be prepared for anything and everything. Naturally, we approached parenthood the same way.

As single people we took full advantage of our freedom to adventure. Through work and vacation I had the opportunity to travel to Asia, the Middle East, and across North America, while Olive worked abroad in Asia. When we were dating and newly married, we travelled to Asia, Europe, Central America, and Africa.

Before we had children, we were intentional about building our marriage as a good foundation in preparation for our future family. This involved getting to know each other, learning to resolve conflict, and developing a clearer vision for our life together. When Alena was born, both Olive and I were 30 years old and had been married for three years and were living just outside of Vancouver,

Canada.

Being first time parents was rough but hardship wasn't unfamiliar territory. We had both faced difficult experiences before. Olive went through burnout that required three years of recovery. I had struggled with depression on and off for 10 years. In a way, these experiences prepared us to face and embrace the challenging emotions that would come with being first-time parents.

In another sense, we were completely unprepared to be parents.

Nothing could have made us ready for the sleep deprivation we experienced or how that impacted the way we functioned and lived. We weren't prepared for the burden and weight of being responsible for someone else's life – especially the life of a tiny and helpless baby. We weren't prepared for how parenting pushed us to grow as individuals, and how it complicated the way we interacted with each other, with our family, and with our friends.

And although everyone told us beforehand that having a child changes your life forever, no matter how much we believed what they told us, we had no idea exactly what that meant.

We would soon find out.

[Olive]

Becoming a mother did not begin with birthing my baby. Motherhood began for me when I decided to be open to the idea of welcoming a new person into my life. Way before our baby was even conceived, I had to make the decision to let go of life as I knew it and to invest myself into another being.

For me, it was not an easy place to arrive at. Tim was open to the change much earlier than I was. I was nervous about the practicalities of caring for an infant. I had very limited prior experience with children. How would I know what to do? I was worried about what would be required of me. Did I have what it would take? I was hesitant about the possibility of losing my figure. I was reluctant to let go of the familiar life, the life of freedom that I'd grown accustomed to. And this world we lived in – this often violent, sad, and problem-ridden world – did I really want to bring a child into this kind of place?

Yet Love beckoned. Love invited me to say, "Yes," to a life that was about more than me. It challenged me to open my heart, to be generous, to dare to help a child grow into an adult and find myself growing up in the process. Love asked me to hope; to believe that raising our next generation with compassion would serve to better the world.

Little did I know how much I would be stretched – physically, mentally, emotionally, and spiritually – or how rich I would become, simply for welcoming a baby.

The Ride of Pregnancy and Birth

1

Impatient

Waiting for a Baby

[Tim]

For as long as I can remember I've loved children. Whenever I got the chance I gravitated towards playing with them: at church, at family functions, or with friends' kids. I reveled in the ability to make them laugh and dreamed of the day that I would be a dad and have kids of my own.

In university I lived in a small dormitory and the dorm parents had two baby girls. Over those years I became one of their favourites. Normally I would take offense to being called, "Dim," but I swelled with pride when two-year old Anya started calling me by that name.

Then I got married to Olive. We both hoped to have children but wanted to have time to build a good foundation in our marriage first. I thought one year would be enough but Olive wanted to wait two years. Since she was the one who would be carrying the child, I decided she could have some say in the decision.

So I waited for my wife to be ready while pretending to be a patient and supportive husband.

There was a tension that I felt. On one hand I treasured the season of marriage where it was "just the two of us." On the other hand I felt impatient at wanting to have a baby sooner rather than later.

When we finally started trying to conceive, we became borderline obsessed with calculating the possible days and times Olive could get pregnant. When each month passed and Olive did not get pregnant, I grew disappointed and increasingly more impatient. But there was only so much control we had over the situation.

[Olive]

Tim had to wait longer than I did for a baby. I felt impatient at times as well, but I don't think I was aware of just how impatient he felt.

There's a term, "Two Week Wait," which refers to the roughly two weeks between when a woman's egg is released and conception is possible to the time pregnancy can be detected. I can't remember if we knew of that term then, but every month those two weeks could not have crept by any slower. My mind would play tricks on me and I would feel little signs and symptoms, only to be disappointed month after month. It got to the point where I would tell Tim, "I'm feeling [insert symptom]. I think this might be the month!" Not wanting to get our hopes up, he would say, "I don't believe it until the test shows you're pregnant."

Waiting to conceive was the hardest time for me because we really could not know whether pregnancy was going to be possible. There was no definite end in sight.

Through the waiting, the thought that helped me address my impatience was that it was ultimately about more than me. Sure, I wanted to have my child now. But our child's life experiences would be shaped and affected by the timing of his or her birth. So perhaps, for our baby's sake, God was allowing him or her to arrive later than we hoped. That, and maybe Tim and I both needed to learn more patience.

2

Elated

Finding Out We Were Pregnant

[Olive]

3:00 am on Tuesday, March 29, 2011: I woke up feeling like I needed to pee. Just before waking up, I dreamt that I was at a hospital getting a pregnancy test done and for some reason there were other people hanging around when the doctor was giving me the instructions. I turned to them and scolded them for so rudely staring at me. "This is important!" I yelled at them. "Stop staring at me and mind your own business!" (When I told Tim about this later, he joked that I was hormonal even in my dreams.)

I had been told that pregnancy tests work best first thing in the morning. My period was late so I decided to try out one of the cheap pregnancy test strips I'd ordered off the Internet. In my groggy state, I stared at the test as one, and then two lines appeared. "You're kidding," I muttered into the quietness. I had not expected this - not this month anyway. The last three weeks had been so stressful and chaotic for us with Tim's grandfather suffering a stroke and being hospitalized and then his parents' emergency visit from Hong Kong. I had also been away for a week taking a course. I thought this month was out in terms of trying for a baby. This was certainly a surprise.

Seeing the first test come out positive, I got out a second, more expensive test to confirm things. Sure enough, a blue "+" showed up in the window, signaling that I was pregnant. Wow, God. Really?

Tim was sleeping blissfully, completely unaware that I had even gotten up. I left him a little note on the bathroom counter along with the positive tests for him to discover in the morning. Crawling back into bed, I tried to sleep. But my thoughts were racing uncontrollably. My heart was thumping like it was about to burst out of my chest. I lay there tossing and turning. Unable to calm myself, I finally woke Tim up and told him the news. Our long awaited dream was coming true!

[Tim]

"Are you awake?" Olive whispered to me in my sleep.

"Maybe," I mumbled, wondering if this was a dream (and waiting to see if ninjas would suddenly appear whirling locally-grown, organic, coconut nun chucks).

Olive paused for a moment. "You're going to be a dad!" she whispered excitedly.

"What? How do you know?" were my exact words. The enormity of the news made me forget how annoyed I was to be woken up in the middle of the night.

She explained to me how she knew. I asked her if she was sure. She told me she used two tests and both of them said yes. The initial shock slowly turned into excitement as the reality sunk in. We were pregnant! We quickly made calculations as to when our baby might be due. We had been trying to get pregnant for eight months now, which apparently was the average amount of time it took for a couple to conceive.

What I felt was a mixture of surprise, elation, relief, and gratitude. We said a prayer of thanks to God and asked Him to protect our baby.

I couldn't sleep after that. Neither could Olive. My mind was racing and my heart was pounding. I was so very delighted.

That would be the first, but definitely not the last, time our baby woke me up in the middle of the night.

3

Fearful

The Possibility of Losing our Baby

[Tim]

Amidst the excitement and joy of expecting a baby was a lurking sense of fear. Deep inside I was afraid of losing our baby, who we treasured dearly.

Months before Olive became pregnant, we found out that friends of ours had experienced a miscarriage. I was heartbroken when I heard the news. I had no idea how to respond when they told us.

From my online search I learned that the highest risk of miscarriage was in the first trimester and occurred in about 15-25% of pregnancies. That percentage was alarmingly high and only fuelled my fear.

For those first few months I lived with a dynamic contrast of emotion – joy and fear. Every night Olive and I would pray that God would keep our baby safe and healthy.

It seemed like that was all we could do.

[Olive]

The fragility of life was never so clear or so pressing to me as during my first trimester of pregnancy. It was as if knowing that I was carrying this new life suddenly brought out the protective instinct in me. I felt responsible for the baby. I wanted to make sure my child had the greatest chance for survival. But there wasn't much I could do to ensure those things. That's probably why I was afraid.

Losing this baby would mean the death of some dreams. It would mean the loss of certain hopes. Most of all, it would mean I'd have to take a good, hard look at my faith and my understanding of who the benevolent God I claimed to believe in was. I wasn't averse to going to that difficult place. I simply hoped I could be spared from it.

After the first trimester was over, I felt a sense of relief. But I was still acutely aware that I had no guarantees for a healthy child. After she was born, there was more relief. But the fear of losing my child never fully went away.

I think that fear I felt during the first trimester was actually a gift; it reminded me to treasure life and take no one for granted.

4

Frustrated

The Alien Invasion

[Olive]

Here's the strange thing: before I became pregnant, I really, really wanted to be pregnant. I longed for it with all my heart. But when I finally was pregnant, I wasn't as happy about it as I thought I would be. Partly, I felt frustrated because I'd lost some measure of predictability and control. I was a recipient of this pregnancy. Yes, Tim and I had done what we could to try to make it happen, but the actual happening of it was not up to me. Without warning, I quickly became at the mercy of my body, its cravings and aversions.

There was no turning back. That can an alarming thought. I had prayed for this. But I had not anticipated the immediate and ongoing effects. I had known it would be uncomfortable, but actually inhabiting a pregnant body was quite another matter. It was frustrating because I couldn't just walk away and take a break from my needy body.

It's funny, too, because for the first six months, I was longing for my belly to start showing so that people would comment on it. And then when I did start to show, I wrestled with feeling like a whale. Toward the end, I felt really enormous and I feared I would never slim down again.

Everyone around me just seemed so excited about our pregnancy. A rare few would ask me how I was feeling. I felt kind of bad for not being as thrilled about things as everyone else seemed to be. I felt like even Tim didn't really get it. It wasn't until I had a couple conversations with some other women who had had similar experiences that I felt like my mixed bag of emotions was valid, normal and acceptable.

Did I want this child? Yes. Was I relieved that we didn't have to go through another month of waiting for my period to show up and asking, "Is this the month?" Yes. Did I look forward to growing our family? Absolutely, yes! Yet, as thankful and glad as I was for this development in our lives, it wasn't as idyllic as I had imagined it to be.

[Tim]

"Do I look fat?" Olive asked me one morning during her last trimester.

I wasn't prepared to answer the question. "Yes," would be the honest answer, but would she feel offended that I thought she was fat? And if I answered "No," would she feel better but then think I was lying? There seemed like no correct way to answer this question. It's a trap, my brain was telling me, but what should I do?

"Yes," I said.

When she gave no response, I quickly said, "No."

Olive furrowed her brows. "I don't know," I added. "However you look, I still love you."

I'm not sure where my answer came from, but it seemed like the right one.

"Why do you ask that question?" I asked her. She stopped to think and then told me that she wondered with all the changes, if she was still loved. It seemed like a no-brainer to me. Of course I still loved her. We both knew she would have changes through the pregnancy. But I think she needed to hear it and to be reminded of it often.

It felt like we were both victims to the changes happening in her body and the demands of the baby. I felt frustrated at how many things Olive needed. She seemed to get grouchy and impatient whenever she was tired, or hungry, or needed to pee. And these things happened constantly.

But I guess as frustrated as I felt, she must have felt that many times more.

5

Shocked

The Birth

[Olive]

It wasn't the way I had envisioned labour. I was supposed to be pacing up and down the hospital corridors and leaning on Tim for each contraction. I had imagined calm music softly playing in the background. I had even put together a playlist specifically for the occasion. It was supposed to be drug-free and although it would be painful, I would be able to handle it. After all, I was made for this.

I had been told beforehand that a birthing plan was more like a wish list. That you could hope for labour to go a certain way but there were no guarantees. I understood that. But still, I was shocked that it ended up happening like this.

This was lying belly up on the hard hospital bed, IV snaking from my left hand, back muscles cramping in discomfort and two bands with attached monitors tightly strapped around my midsection. *This* was not being allowed to eat or drink, save for a few sips of water now and then. *This* was getting my pulse and temperature checked every hour. All while the contractions coursed through my body in increasing intensity.

In retrospect, I wish I hadn't prayed for my water to break first. I had wanted a clear signal that labour was beginning. But what I did not know was that once the amniotic sac ruptured, if we wanted to minimize risk of infection, we would have 24 hours to birth the baby.

My water broke at 6:29 am on Monday morning, three days past the due date. The entire day had been spent praying that my body would begin contractions in earnest on its own. By 6:29 pm, I was still having inconsistent contractions. My doctor recommended that I be given the hormone oxytocin to speed things up.

I checked into the hospital at 8:00 pm and a few hours later, as the nurse started administering the hormone via IV, I became prisoner to the bed.

As the labour unfolded and I realized this was going to happen very differently than what I would have chosen, I knew I had a decision to make. I could continue to grasp at any semblance of control. Or I could let go and surrender. I decided to trust.

It was a humbling experience. From the outside, I had nurses probing me and monitoring me. From the inside, the contractions would ride like ever increasing waves. By 4:45 am, my body began to push involuntarily, despite them having just checked me 15 minutes before and finding me only 5 cm dilated. The medical personnel were alarmed as it wasn't safe for me to push until I was 10 cm dilated. They said I should consider getting some drugs to take the edge off of the pain and hopefully allow my body to relax and stop pushing. I said ok.

The drug helped to relax me in between contractions, but whenever the contractions came, my body continued to push. I felt like I was fighting to hold my baby in.

I felt powerless. And a little fuzzy-brained.

In fact, the remainder of labour became a bit of a blur so I will let Tim tell the rest of the story.

[Tim]

"I can see the head," the nurse said calmly.

I jerked up, awake all of a sudden. WHAAT? How did this happen so fast? I looked down and sure enough I saw the top of my baby's head. There was so much hair! I stared in disbelief, so stunned I didn't know what to do.

"The doctor's not going to make it," the nurse announced in a very matter-of-fact tone, like it was no big deal. Instantly, my heart rate tripled.

"You know how to deliver a baby right?" I half-jokingly, half-seriously asked the nurse. I added a nervous laugh to try to hide my panic, "Ha. Ha."

"Yes, of course," she replied.

I looked over at Olive, she was sweating and in pain. Immediately I remembered our pre-natal class and what I was supposed to do to help my wife.

"Breathe slowly," I said to Olive while demonstrating slow and steady breaths.

"Stop blowing into my face," Olive replied crossly.

"Oops, sorry," I responded, feeling like an idiot for making things worse.

I took out my smartphone and started video recording what was happening. We had disagreed beforehand whether or not to record this moment. Olive wasn't sure she wanted to watch or remember this painful experience. I convinced her that we should record it so that she could have the option to watch it. (Weeks after the birth, Olive did end up watching the videos and was glad for them because she had very little recollection of what happened.)

After a few pushes from Olive the baby popped out.

"It's a girl."

With all my waiting for the baby you would think I would be ready for this moment. But I wasn't. In fact, I was more shocked than anything.

The nurses quickly cleaned up our little girl and placed her on Olive's chest.

"What's her name?" one of the nurses asked. Olive and I looked at each other and smiled.

"Alena." I said. "Alena Joy Chan."

I stared in disbelief at the tiny 6 lb 15 oz baby, lying on her mother. It felt dreamlike. Alena's eyes were open, blinking slowly, staring out into the world. It felt like time slowed, allowing us to appreciate the beauty of new life.

Then I noticed a funny smell, a smell I would become very familiar with. Alena had pooped on Olive. It was like she was marking her territory.

The doctor soon arrived and helped Olive "deliver" the placenta. This was the part that no one warned us about. (The placenta is an organ that stores all the nutrition that is relayed to the baby.) This part was even more painful for Olive than delivering the baby. Once the placenta was out, the doctor also had to stitch Olive up because she had a 2nd degree tear. This was also very painful. I remember cringing the entire time, holding Olive's hand, watching helplessly as she endured the pain. My love and respect for Olive grew significantly that night. She was amazing and I was extremely proud of her.

Finally it was over, and the nurses cleaned up and left the three of us alone.

I turned to Olive and said, "You did it."

"We did it," she said smiling tiredly at me.

Olive and I looked at each other and then at Alena. "Hello Alena, welcome to the world. We love you."

The Ride

As Parents

6

Captivated

Aww... She's So Cute!

[Tim]

"Welcome home," I said to Allie. It seemed so surreal to be back at home with our little one.

It was amazing how long I could stare at a newborn baby. I got lost in time watching Allie. I never imagined I could use the word "cute" so many times in one day.

Everything she did was adorable: when she blinked, when she sneezed, when she had the hiccups, and even when she farted (but I drew the line at poop; her poop was definitely not cute). I loved watching her yawn, as she opened her tiny little mouth wide and stretched out her arms. I loved it when she wrapped her miniature hand around my fingers and I wondered how such a tiny person could have such a strong grip.

By the end of the first week, I had taken hundreds of

photos and videos of Allie. I was like the paparazzi, sitting in her room with my camera pointed at her while she was sleeping. With any movement she made I took a dozen photos. Not that the photos were all worth keeping. I was like a beginner video game player who just pressed all the buttons hoping something good will happen.

Everything my baby did was so fascinating. Perhaps it was the novelty of having a baby for the first time. Perhaps it was that she was so tiny and beautiful. Perhaps it was that I had wanted to be a father for so many years and it had finally happened. Whatever it was, those first precious days were full of joy and wonder.

[Olive]

It took some getting used to, this being a parent thing. I remember one night when Allie was about a month old, the sound of crying woke me up from my sleep. "Who brought a crying baby into our house?!" I wondered. I quickly realized that baby was mine.

It surprised me, how much I loved watching her. Her tiny flailing arms and legs, her delicate fingers and sweetpea toes. I loved the way multiple expressions would flicker across her face in a span of minutes. More than anything, it was her pout that I loved the most. Her little lips would start quivering and then, right before she began to full out cry, we'd see it – the cutest pout in the whole wide world. We attempted to catch the moment on camera so many times. A couple times we even purposely let her stay hungry for a few minutes longer just to elicit that pout!

Alena was the first newborn that I really interacted with.

I doubt any other experience will ever replicate that feeling of being so completely captivated by one person. And nothing will come close to the feeling of wonder of realizing that this person came from me.

7

Hopeful

What Shall We Name This Little One?

[Tim]

Being planners, Olive and I started the process of naming our baby half a year before the due date. We started by brainstorming names we liked.

Girls' names were easier for us to agree on. But all the boys' names we came up with were vetoed, either because I knew a jerk with that name or Olive's friends had given their son that name. We were relieved when the ultrasound revealed that we were most likely going to have a girl.

We wanted to give our child a meaningful name so that in times of uncertainty, she could reflect on it and be reminded of who she was called to be. We also thought through possible nicknames and tested out how the names sounded with our last name, "Chan." Slowly, we whittled our initial list of 13 names down to three.

Then we started thinking about middle names. Olive's good friend grew up not liking her first name so everyone called her by her middle name. Just in case our daughter did not like the name we chose for her (for whatever reason), we thought it would be a good idea that she had a middle name to use as a backup.

By the time her due date arrived, we both had agreed on a top choice for a girl's name. Olive wanted to wait to see the baby to make the final decision, and I agreed. Moments after the baby was born, Olive and I looked at each other and both somehow knew that we wanted to name her Alena Joy Chan (which was our first choice).

The meaning of Alena (pronounced a-LAY-nah) was "light." Our hope was that our daughter would be a light in the world, shining in times of darkness, difficulty or confusion. We liked how her first name and middle name flowed together, plus we hoped that she would be a person full of joy. We hoped for her to have a deep, lasting joy that was more than the happiness that was dependent on circumstances. Our hope was that Alena's joy would come from God and would not fade. Plus, we liked how she could have the nicknames of "Allie," "Lena," or "Lainey."

[Olive]

Being Chinese, we thought it would also be appropriate to give Alena a Chinese name to remind her of her heritage and to add more dimension to the meaning of her name. It would not be on any official documents, but she would know it and the family would know it.

The hardest part was coming up with one. Having

grown up in Canada, Tim and I have basic, functional Chinese – we know how to talk about food and weather, hardly the level of fluency required to name a child. Thankfully, both sets of our parents knew Chinese, so we involved them in the naming process.

When Allie was about three weeks old, we invited all four of her grandparents over for dinner with the purpose of brainstorming a Chinese name. There were many things to take into consideration. Chinese is a complex language and choosing two complementing characters was not simple. The conversation that evening went back and forth as each of our parents gave their suggestions and the other three gave their feedback. Finally, we had a list of 19 agreed upon characters to choose from.

It was a tiring and somewhat frustrating process. We ended up not being able to decide on a name that night. But over the course of the next couple weeks, Tim and I settled on "Yun," which meant "joy from the heart," and "Chi," which was the character for "loving kindness." The last character was shared with my own Chinese name. It seemed especially meaningful to be able to pass a bit of my legacy on to Alena in that way.

8

Overwhelmed

A Million Things to Learn in a Day

[Olive]

The Cambridge Dictionary defines "crash course" as "a course that teaches you a lot of basic facts in a very short time."[1] In the weeks following Allie's birth, we were involuntarily enrolled in a crash course on baby care. The alarming thing was, they weren't only facts that we were learning, they were life skills.

There was so much to learn all at once that we somewhat unconsciously became selective about what we focused on. In the midst of trying to figure out how to feed, burp, bathe and swaddle the baby, we neglected to dress her. It wasn't until she was about four days old that our relatives and friends started commenting on our photos and saying things like, "Why isn't she wearing any clothes in any of your pictures?" We were working so hard on perfecting our swaddling skills and getting enough skin-to-skin contact during the frequent nursing sessions that we just turned up the heat in our apartment and "dressed" her in a diaper and a blanket. After all, that's what they did at the hospital. It also felt surprisingly daunting to have to decide on whether to dress her in a onesie, sleeper, or kimono.

Diapering was a whole other matter in itself. Before Allie was born, we had decided to go with a cloth diapering service (they'd provide us with clean diapers each week and take away the soiled ones). We were excited about this option because babies that used cloth diapers tended to potty-train earlier (an exciting thought), and using cloth diapers was better for the environment. But when we got home with our little bundle of flailing arms and legs, we promptly decided we'd tackle cloth diapering later and figure out basic diapering with disposables first!

There were so many things to learn in that initial month. And although we had done some preparation work before Allie was born, nothing could have prepared us for the onslaught of new skills that were required of us. It was overwhelming. Perhaps all the more because we were trying to figure them out while being sleep deprived.

[Tim]

In most areas of life I can take a course or practice a bit to prepare myself before starting something new. For example:
- Driving lessons before getting my driver's license,
- Time to study before taking an exam,
- Training before starting a new job.

Unfortunately there was no such thing when it came to being a new parent. This made me especially nervous because I am the type of person that likes to be prepared for everything. This, I think, is the reason I have recurring nightmares of starting an exam with the feeling of panic because I had not gone to any classes the entire semester or even read the textbook.

I felt so ill-equipped in caring for our newborn. How were we supposed to feed her? Bathe her? Carry her? Rock her to sleep?

When it came to swaddling a baby in a blanket, the baby is supposed to be wrapped up like a burrito. The first few times I tried swaddling her it looked more like a messy wonton.

The first time we bathed Alena it must have taken us 20 minutes. I was grateful that my father-in-law had taken a video of the nurse showing us how to bathe the baby at the hospital. At the time we had been up for about two days straight and nothing really registered any more.

Clipping a baby's teeny tiny nails was the hardest thing in the world. I never sweat more than when I had to cut Allie's nails. I would hold her delicate fingers and use a miniature nail clipper to trim her smaller-than-watermelon-seed sized nails, trying my very best to cut only her nails and not her fingers.

The first few times went okay and I started feeling like I was getting the hang of things. Then one time I accidentally clipped her nail and her finger. Blood started squirting everywhere (at least that's how I remember it in the traumatized version of my memory). While Allie was wailing in pain, tiny beads of tears streaming down her face, I tried to stop the bleeding. This is when we discovered the handy invention of spray-on bandages (because normal bandages were too giant for her tiny fingers).

No one ever warned us that as new parents we would have this near-impossible responsibility. Learning to clip a baby's nails with precision should be part of prenatal classes. They should stick little pieces of rice on a water balloon filled with red water, and the to-be parents should have to use a tiny nail clipper to remove the pieces of rice. If they accidentally puncture the water balloon, the red water would spray everywhere. On top of that, someone should cry and scream directly in their ears for five minutes straight.

On second thought, I see why this exercise isn't done. It would freak out parents-to-be too much.

Somehow we made it through those first few weeks of feeling overwhelmed, learning as we went. I felt sorry for Allie, because she was literally our guinea pig as we practiced caring for her.

9

Heroic

Rocking Allie to Sleep

[Tim]

We were told that a baby cries the most during her sixth week of life. I was mentally preparing for this week, ready to step up my daddy duties and turn on my superhero mode. Olive was still recovering from labour, so I told her that I would put Allie to sleep every night.

It was like a switch that was flipped. When the sixth week started, Allie all of a sudden began to cry for extended periods of time in the evening. So every night starting from 9 pm I would hold Allie for two to three hours, until she would finally drift off. After one evening of experimenting with the most comfortable way to do this, I discovered I was able to sit on the couch and rest Allie on a pillow on my lap. When she cried, I would either put a pacifier in her mouth or rock her a bit, until she stopped and fell back asleep.

To prevent myself from falling asleep while rocking Allie

(a fear of mine), I rented Season 6 of the thrilling TV series "24." Watching this definitely kept me awake.

That week I watched the entire season of "24," which consisted of twenty-four one-hour episodes. There were times when I wondered if Allie could hear the sounds of shouting, gunshots, and bombs exploding, and whether it would negatively impact her. I turned the volume down and put on the subtitles, trying to convince myself that the sound of gunshots might be soothing. Good thing Allie was pretty immune to noise at that age.

And Olive, bless her soul, made me feel like a superhero for doing this, which made me feel great. My wife really was a genius and knew how to affirm me (and get me to do stuff).

I actually looked forward to those 2-3 hours every night, because I really wanted to find out why special agent Jack Bauer had gone rogue and seemed to be hijacking the US special services in their hunt for Russian terrorists threatening to use weapons of mass destruction to kill thousands of innocent people, while holding Allie and getting her to sleep.

[Olive]

Sure I was slightly concerned about exposing my infant to the sounds of violence and suspenseful music. But I was just glad I didn't have to stay up with a crying baby every night.

And yes, Tim is my hero.

10

Shaken

Allie's First Vaccinations

[Olive]

When Allie was two months young, we brought her to our family doctor for a check up and her first set of vaccinations. After taking her measurements, the doctor explained that she was going to administer four sets of vaccines, one being an oral vaccine and the other three being injections. I felt a bit nervous, but our doctor was experienced and we trusted her. After all, how bad could it be?

She started off with the oral vaccine, which Allie accepted fine. And then she laid our baby down on the examination table and instructed me to hold onto our baby's legs while she gave the shots.

Nothing could have prepared me for that moment when she thrust the needle into Allie's thigh. The doctor might as well have driven a stake into my heart. Allie, of course, screamed and thrashed about. And I desperately tried to keep my composure. Within seconds, it was over and my baby was safely back in my arms. A couple minutes later, she was cooing happily. I, however, felt shaken and all rattled up on the inside.

When we got to the car, I couldn't hold it in any longer. I wept.

I wept for all the pain Allie would endure in her life. I wept for all the pain I would inflict upon my daughter. I wept for all the pain I would be helpless in protecting her from. I wept for all the times she would look at me in confusion, not understanding that the pain was for her good and necessary for her growth. I wept because she was only two months old and there was still a very long road ahead.

And then I told Tim that he could have the dubious honour of holding Allie for all future vaccines.

[Tim]

Taking Allie to get her vaccinations seemed necessary and routine for me. Yes, I knew it would hurt. But I knew Allie had a short memory and would recover quickly from pain. Plus, she was already always crying, so what was a little bit more crying.

When it was time for her 4-month shots, Olive had already informed me that I would need to hold Allie for all her remaining vaccinations. This wasn't one of those things that was up for discussion, so I just accepted it as part of my role as a father.

When the first needle went into Allie's little thigh she screamed in pain. I continued holding her down and once the vaccines were all administered, I hastily picked her up and calmed her. She was all sweaty and sobbing, with snot running and tears streaming down her face. Poor girl. But in a matter of minutes she was fine.

Then I turned to console my poor wife. It took longer for her to recover. Seeing Allie get shots always broke Olive's heart a little. I hugged Olive and told her that she had done a good job, and that she could have a cookie for being so brave.

11

Fortunate

Sleep Training the Baby

[Olive]

Parenthood often felt (and continues to feel) like one grand experiment. There were many theories for every topic related to child rearing, but would it work for our child? There was only one way to find out.

I clearly remember the night we started sleep training Allie. Even though it was 2 am, I was quite alert because curiosity had my adrenaline pumping. I had read that if a baby woke at the same time each night, it was out of habit. But if the baby woke at random times, it was because of a growth spurt and she was hungry. Allie had been waking at 2 am pretty consistently for a couple weeks so I thought it was safe to attribute it to habit rather than hunger. I was excited to test the theory out.

That night, Allie cried right on time and I went into her room to get her. I remember bringing her pacifier, hovering over her crib, picking her up and putting the pacifier in her mouth.

I held my breath and waited. Was she going to realize there was no milk and continue fussing? Surprisingly, she settled down and soon fell asleep. I gently laid her in her crib and crept back into bed, inwardly rejoicing.

I had also read that it takes a baby anywhere from three nights to a few weeks to sleep train. The next night, I armed myself with the pacifier again. But to our surprise, it wasn't necessary. Allie only needed one night to break her habit.

Successfully sleep training felt like the first big milestone for us as a family of three. Many of our friends were not as fortunate as we were in the sleep department. However, what no one warned us of was the vengeance of sleep regressions – which we would find out about soon enough.

[Tim]

When Allie was 10 weeks old, Olive and I decided that we would sleep train her – or at least attempt to. To prepare, we read books and blog posts on the subject. ("We," meaning, "Olive." This is an area where I rely on my wife's strengths. She loves information and devours books. She is what some people call a "knowledge specialist.")

I was unsure of trying to sleep train our baby so soon. Perhaps it was because the concept was completely new to me, or perhaps the idea of our baby sleeping through the night seemed too good to be true. I worried that Allie would go hungry and starve – it seemed a bit cruel to take away one of her meals all of a sudden.

So it seemed like a miracle to me that the sleep training

worked. I'd never felt so good waking up at 5:30 am in my life. But it was glorious. Seven whole hours of consecutive sleep.

We tried not to brag to our friends, but it was too hard not to. Many people asked us how our baby was sleeping and we would happily answer that she slept through the night. They would ask how this could be possible. And we would say that we were genius parents and should win some sort of international award for our sleep training successes. Then our parent friends would tell us that their 1 year old still woke up two to three times every night no matter what sleep training methods they tried, and we would try to tone things down.

The truth is that we felt very fortunate that Allie was a good sleeper and could take no credit for this happening. God probably knew that we were wimps and had terrible attitudes when we were sleep deprived and decided to spare Allie from this.

12

Proud

Allie's First

[Olive]

There's a profound sense of wonder and joy in witnessing a baby's development. It's like you get to re-discover the world through her. To see her gain mastery over her body, to watch her brain make connections, to observe her growing social awareness, these are all causes for delight in a parent.

It feels odd to say it, but I am extremely proud of my baby. I am proud of who she is. She hasn't done much in her short life, but still, there is a sense of wanting to show her off to the world.

Every developmental milestone Allie reaches is a cause for celebration. I remember feeling so thrilled when as a newborn she would turn her head to look at the lights. And then she found her fingers. And then she found her toes. They were basic skills, but there was a sense of satisfaction in seeing her become more of the human she was created to be. In a way, we felt like she had succeeded and we wanted to applaud that.

As we grow up, we often lose sight of how valuable we are. I hope Alena will always remember that she is worth celebrating.

[Tim]

Allie stood on her own the other day. When I first saw it I was shocked. When did she learn to do this?! My baby's growing up! This is amazing!

She just stood there keenly observing her book in her little hands, not even aware that she was standing on her own, unassisted, for the first time in her life. She looked over at me nonchalantly like she was saying, "Yeah, I'm standing, but it's no big deal."

Meanwhile Olive and I were going crazy and clapping our hands with delight, calling my parents and brother and sister and telling them the great news about how marvelous, wonderful and simply amazing Allie was. I wanted to award her a trophy that said "Allie's first time standing," and put the date and time on it, to commemorate this milestone. We would place the trophy on our bookcase which was full of other trophies we had made for Allie, including:

- First time she slept through the night.
- First time she waved.
- First time she ate peaches.
- First time she touched snow.
- First time she pooped in the shape of a heart (with

accompanying photo).

All Allie did was stand on her own for 2 seconds… which was AMAZING!! And people wonder why the trophy company is on my speed dial.

13

Love

The Most Important Thing

[Tim]

Sometimes I sneak into Allie's room just to watch her sleep. I gaze at her breathing in and out, her little chest rising and falling. It's so amazing how much I love her. This little baby has stolen my heart.

New parenthood is full of chaos – a crying baby, dirty diapers, endless laundry, and sleepless nights. Many times I question whether or not we are making the best decisions for Allie. During those times of uncertainty I remind myself about the most important thing about parenting: love. What is even more important than us loving our daughter is the fact that she knows that she is loved.

Recently, we watched the Oscar-winning movie "The Help." I was inspired by what Abileen, one of the helpers, repeated to one of the children she was caring for, "You is Beautiful. You is Smart. You is Important."

Whenever I get the chance I tell Allie:
    "You are beautiful.
    You are valued.
    And you are very loved."

I repeat it over and over again as I hold her:
    "You are beautiful.
    You are valued.
    And you are very loved."

Remember this Alena Joy Chan.
Remember this every time you feel like a failure.
Remember this every time you feel hurt.
Remember this every time you feel ashamed of yourself.
Remember this every time you feel ugly.
Remember this every time you feel unloved.

You are loved.
You are very loved.
Loved by your dad. Loved by your mom. Loved by your family. Loved by God.

[Olive]

If there is only one thing I manage to teach my child, I want it to be this: that she is deeply loved. The extent to which she understands this truth is the extent to which she can live in fullness and freedom.

I want her to know that she is enough. That her life matters. I want her to be so sure of her own value that she can accept both her strengths and weaknesses and she doesn't need to prove anything. Then she can have compassion for herself and compassion for others.

So I pray to this end and I parent to this end. I try to tell her as often as I can, through words and actions, that I love her. But where it truly begins is within my own self; I first need to know that I am fully loved.

The amazing thing is this: As much as I want her to know she is loved, her gaze tells me that I am loved.

14

Bored

The Challenge of Staying Present

[Tim]

Sometimes I get bored with my baby. It's not that she isn't interesting, but the initial novelty and excitement of having a baby wears out after a while.

What I hear myself telling my friends is that I like working part-time because I get to spend more time with Allie. But what I see myself doing is zoning out and ignoring Allie when I'm with her.

It's easy to focus on technology rather than paying attention to my baby. I think it's because with technology, I have complete control. My laptop or smartphone does what I want it to do (for the most part), whereas my baby only occasionally does what I want her to do.

It's easy to get bored when reading, "Bunny Eats Lunch," 13 times in a row to Allie. But she made it clear that she wanted me to continue by nodding her head and giving a baby grunt of approval, "Mm." This particular book's plot is about how the bunny eats carrots and potatoes for lunch. The climax is when the bunny burps at the end. (Don't everyone go and buy the book all at once now.)

Sometimes to amuse myself I change the story. The bunny is eating pizza and frozen yogurt (a.k.a. froyo). The bunny has explosive diarrhea because pizza and froyo is a bad combination. The bunny sneaks off to play mahjong with Elmo, Winnie the Pooh, and Justin Bieber on the weekends.

Being a parent to a baby challenges me to practice being present and to enjoy the life that is in front of me. To do this I must fight the temptation to do something more exciting and more engaging (i.e. attempting to be productive by checking email or watching sports highlights).

Author Brené Brown says "Joy comes to us in moments— ordinary moments. We risk missing out on joy when we get too busy chasing down the extraordinary." As long as I am a parent, I will remind myself to be grateful for the ordinary moments in life.

[Olive]

It seems that my daughter came equipped with radar. She knows when I've mentally left the room. Every time I flick on my phone to check my email or take a quick peek at Facebook, she will either vocally make a fuss or physically come pull on my leg. It's like she's saying, "Mommy! Come back to me!"

Most of the time, I try to be present and attentive to her. But sometimes my brain wants a break. When I've spent the last ten minutes singing the Alphabet Song or reading the same darned book seven times in a row, I want to do something more exciting.

I recently explained to a close friend of mine that spending time with a baby is somewhat akin to spending time with a pet. You know they like you, you're not quite sure how much they understand and it's very much a one-sided conversation.

It's tempting to space out every once in a while and look for something more entertaining, especially since everything is so conveniently accessible on my smartphone. But I don't want to send my child the message that this rectangular, black gadget is more important to me than she is. Constantly looking at my phone is not the posture I want her to remember me by. So I make it a point to be completely available to her when we're playing together. And I try to think of creative activities and games that both of us can enjoy.

It requires more of me, but if I'm not the one to love her and give her my full attention, who is?

15

Resourceful

How to Pee While Holding a Baby

[Olive]

It was a beautiful Saturday in July. Tim had been asked to give the homily at our friends' wedding. Having arrived a little early so that Tim could prepare, I fed Allie some milk and watched as other guests slowly arrived.

Suddenly, I realized I needed to use the bathroom. There was no one around that I knew so I resigned myself to the fact that I would need to bring Allie with me. I picked her up and headed down two flights of stairs into the basement, where the washrooms were located.

I entered the stall, breathed a sigh of gratitude that I was wearing a skirt and put Allie on my lap. It actually wasn't as difficult as I'd thought it would be. I had been faced with a dilemma and I had conquered it.

I emerged from that bathroom wishing I could brag to somebody. But really, who would want to hear a stranger tell them, "I just peed while holding my baby!"?

[Tim]

One time I went to the mall with Allie. This particular time I decided not to bring the stroller or baby carrier. It would be a quick stop and I would just carry Allie.

When I went inside I felt the sudden urge to pee. The question was, "What do I do with my baby while I pee?" There was no way I was putting her on the dirty public bathroom floor. I also could not leave her outside. Normally I would use the family bathroom, where I could place Allie on the change table, but the line up for the family bathroom was very long.

Since nature was calling urgently, I decided the only thing to do was to hold Allie with one arm and to do my business with the other.

As I stood there at the urinal a few things started going through my mind:

- First, why did I order an extra large iced tea at lunch and drink it all?
- Second, why did I not work out more? (My arm was starting to feel very weak.)
- Third, what the heck is Olive feeding our baby that she is so darn heavy?

The muscles in my left arm started trembling and I started to panic because I had no plan B. I had obviously not thought this through. What did other parents do in this situation? This scenario could potentially end in disaster.

Maybe I could ask the guy beside me to hold my baby, "Excuse me sir, could you pick up my baby? My arm is about to give up and I still have a lot of pee to get rid of. She'll definitely start crying because you are a stranger, but I'll be finished soon. Please… it's an emergency…"

I could see the guy look awkwardly at me, feigning that he did not understand English and start walking away quickly. That's what I would have done if someone asked me the same question.

Thankfully my weak arm somehow managed to support my baby's weight while I finished peeing. I was so relieved (pun intended).

My left arm was sore for two days after that, a reminder never to attempt something so foolish again.

16

Loved

The Sweetest Headbutt in the World

[Tim]

Allie hugged me goodbye before I left for work this morning. It was the first time she's ever done this. Instead of hugging with her arms, she hugged with her head so it was more like a head butt.

It was the sweetest headbutt I'd received in my entire life.

[Olive]

Allie learning to hug was a momentous development. Before that, all her affections had been responses to us – she'd smile because we smiled at her, or laughed because we did something to make her laugh. But her hugs, they were initiated by her.

The other night, we were out at dinner with family and

Allie was sitting next to me. Out of the blue, she wrapped herself around my arm and burrowed her head into my shoulder. She was giving me a hug!

When she saw everyone taking out their cameras and oohing and aahing, she kept repeating it. In that moment, I felt like I had won the lottery. She really did love me.

The Ride
As Individuals

17

Despair

I Really Want to Escape

[Olive]

During the first month of motherhood, I often wondered why I ever wanted a child in the first place.

I was weary. I felt stuck in a never-ending, three-hour cycle: wake up, pump/feed the baby, wash the equipment, eat, try to sleep and wake up to repeat it all over again. When was I supposed to fit in a shower? Or talk to Tim? Or simply hold and enjoy my baby?

I felt like a walking zombie. Life was a haze. I felt thankful that Tim and my parents were around to care for Alena. I could barely care for myself. I felt like I was in a constant state of despair.

I was sick of living in a pain-riddled body. Recovering from the birth was slow and painful. It hurt to sit, stand, or go to the washroom. My back muscles ached from stooping over all day and night.

I was sick of all the extra attention my boobs needed. There were more potential complications with breastfeeding than I ever thought possible. Mastitis (a terribly painful infection) and thrush (another type of infection) were constant threats. No one warned me of this, but milk could get clogged in there way too easily. And it would hurt. A lot. And then there was the general pain of having more milk than I could physically contain, which also came with the mess of leaking.

I thought motherhood was supposed to be something fun, something to look forward to. It was more like being a walking pillar of pain.

I felt trapped; like I had no more to give. Yet I could not escape from the relentless needs of this little dependent person. I desperately wanted a break. But even if I got a break from her, I couldn't leave my body. It felt hopeless.

[Tim]

Olive often shared with me about how weary she felt. Not just during the first month of motherhood, but all throughout the first year of Allie's life. There was a hopelessness I noticed in her eyes and on her face, like she could see no end to her tiredness. I could see that having to care for our baby and care for herself was taking a toll on her.

I'm concerned that my wife may burn out or go into depression. I'm concerned for myself, because I'm not sure what more I can do – I feel tired too. I'm concerned for Allie, because she may not be getting the best care she deserves from her overtired parents.

Often I feel unhappy. Unhappy that my wife feels so many "negative" emotions related to being a mother. I'm afraid that she'll decide she doesn't want another child (and I do... at least most days). I'm afraid that her negative emotions may get passed on to Allie, and Allie will end up having an unhappy childhood.

I wish parenting could be butterflies and cupcakes and happy good times all the time. But unfortunately that is not the case.

18

Resentful

The Interruption of Freedom

[Olive]

It's kind of annoying how our baby has more power over our lives than she realizes. If she is happy, I feel great. If she is unhappy, my emotions go down with her. How early she ends up sleeping tonight decides whether Tim and I finally get to watch that movie we borrowed from the library. I can't decorate our home however I want to any more. I have to keep her safety in mind. Even my wardrobe choices are defined by how functional the clothes are when I'm carrying her.

Life with a baby also means continual change. I feel like we're constantly responding; constantly evaluating what her needs are for the moment and how we can meet them. And because she is changing, our needs are changing as well.

Sometimes it feels like I invited chaos to live with us. This is hard for me. I like predictability and routine. I like stability. I also like to have control over my own life. At times I resent the interruption of autonomy.

Being a parent is possibly life's greatest lesson in selflessness. I can no longer do whatever I fancy. For the time being, I will choose to let Allie's needs take precedence and adjust my life in response to her. The challenge is how to do this graciously.

[Tim]

We had to plan our lives around the baby's schedule. It dictated our lives. Sometimes I felt resentful – not at the baby, but at the situation we found ourselves in.

Between Olive needing to pump every 3 hours, Allie needing to eat every 2-3 hours, Allie's nap times, Allie's diaper changes, Olive needing to eat every 3 hours (because pumping was making her especially hungry), and our regular meals, our days became a scheduling nightmare. This definitely put my logistics university degree to use. I created a spreadsheet with the day's schedule in 30-minute intervals and posted it on our fridge. This was our daily regimen that we would strictly follow. If we disobeyed the schedule, the result was a grumpy wife (because she was hungry, tired, or uncomfortably full of milk) or a crying baby (because she was hungry, tired, or needed to be changed).

This schedule left no space for any social life or spontaneity. I was constantly turning down invitations from friends to play poker, attend parties, or go out for dinner. To say that I felt restricted is an understatement. It was like I had been thrown into maximum-security prison where they let me outside for 10 minutes a day to breathe some fresh air, and then threw me back into the seemingly endless cycle of feeding, diaper changing, baby rocking, bottle washing, laundry, cooking, dishes, and catching up on sleep.

19

Naïve

Our First Vacation With the Baby

[Olive]

"How was I so dumb?" I asked over and over. Vacationing with a baby was not at all what I'd expected. I berated myself for being so naïve as to think it would be relaxing like all our previous vacations.

For a first road trip with Allie, Seattle seemed to be a manageable destination. We had booked a vacation rental to share with our friends, Dave and Maria, who were flying in from Michigan. They were expecting their first child so we figured it would be a great opportunity to hang out with them and give them an inside look into what their lives would soon be like.

Our first mistake was opting for the suite at the top of the house. It was pretty, but we hadn't factored in all the STUFF we'd have to schlep up three flights of stairs because of our little princess. Tim must have made at least four or five trips just to get all of it up there.

Our second mistake was opting for a suite in a house with other suites. That first night, Allie woke up and cried. Every. Single. Hour. Normally, it's hard enough when the baby doesn't sleep. But since we were in a house where sound travelled quite well, we were petrified that our baby would disrupt all the other people's holidays. Tim and I were on super-alert mode all night long. We were all exhausted just in time for our first full day of sightseeing.

My biggest mistake was simply expecting an easy vacation in the first place. It turned out to be hard, hard work. It was all the demands of caring for a baby at home minus the familiarity and comforts of home.

I concluded after that visit to Seattle that there actually was no such thing as a vacation with a baby. You can take trips with a baby. But it's no vacation. That's probably why we never took Allie on another trip that year.

[Tim]

My experience of our Seattle trip was not as terrible as Olive's. The main reason was that I function better with less sleep than she does.

Two things about the trip made it difficult. First, the lack of sleep all of us experienced, which is why we nicknamed this vacation, "Sleepless in Seattle." I seriously wondered if we brought the wrong baby on vacation with us. Allie, who had been sleeping through the night for three months up to that point, suddenly had to be rocked to sleep only to wake up every hour or two crying.

The second thing was that Allie developed stranger

anxiety on this trip. In the past, we could let anyone hold Allie and she would be fine. But on the trip, we couldn't even leave Allie for a few moments without her crying. This meant that our friends could not help us watch or babysit Allie (which we had been counting on).

What ended up happening was that some of us saw more of Seattle than others. All five of us would sightsee and eat together for one-third of the day. Then we would drop off Olive, who needed to rest. Dave, Maria, Allie, and I would continue sightseeing for another one-third of the day. Then Allie and I would return home, and Dave and Maria would continue on their own.

We were grateful that our friends were very accommodating. I enjoyed spending time with them and it was nice to get out of the city and travel.

Seeing the toll this trip took on Olive made me reconsider travelling with Allie while she was still a baby. In the future, if we were to travel, I think we'd go with people that Allie was familiar with. That way, at least we would have some backup babysitters so we could take some breaks.

20

Bittersweet

Leaving the Baby with the Sitter

[Tim]

When my parents come to visit, we try to take advantage of this and have them babysit. We tell them we're giving them quality alone time with their granddaughter. Our true motivation is that we really want to get out of the house to go on a much-needed date.

My parents must think that we are really uptight because in the days leading up to their babysitting time I am constantly telling them what to do and what not to do. This list includes things like:

- Don't let her snack before mealtimes.
- Don't feed her things with sugar in it.
- Don't let her eat things off the floor (i.e. dust bunnies).
- Don't let her watch too many videos on your tablet.

And just in case they don't remember the 101 rules for

taking care of Allie, I write them down.

When we finally leave, it's nice having Olive sit in the front seat of the car with me – for once I don't have to feel like a chauffeur. We go out for dinner and then a movie. It's wonderful to have an uninterrupted conversation with Olive. But throughout the evening I find my thoughts going back to Allie and wondering how she is doing. Is she crying? Did my parents remember to feed her? During dinner Olive says she misses Allie, and I say I do too. She breaks out her phone and we watch videos of our baby and laugh. It only makes us miss Allie more.

It's a funny feeling leaving my baby with babysitters. I feel free and I worry at the same time. It's a worried freedom.

[Olive]

"Making the decision to have a child is momentous. It is to decide forever to have your heart go walking around outside your body," observed author Elizabeth Stone. We realize this every time we leave Allie in the care of someone else.

The very first time we left Allie, it was for one hour. She was five days old. My sister-in-law, Tiff, and her husband, Simon, were over and I was craving a Peppermint Mocha. Tim and I went on a mini-date and walked across the street to Starbucks. We both kept checking our phones in case they texted us.

I'm not sure who was more nervous that first time – us, or the babysitters. Somehow we all survived.

During the first six months of Allie's life, it was actually pretty easy to leave her with a sitter. She wasn't particular about who fed her and anyone could put her to sleep. We could have gone out more, really, except for the fact that I had only 3 or 4 hours of being out before my boobs would insist that I go home to pump. That, and I would rather sleep.

Then Allie developed stranger anxiety and would cry when left with anyone else. Over time, it got slightly better, but many times I felt sorry for whoever was babysitting. They often seemed to be at a loss for what to do with our crying baby. And when we got home, I felt like I needed to apologize for leaving them with an inconsolable pair of lungs.

For all the worry, having time alone with Tim was always refreshing. It was a treat to speak normally without nonsensical babble or interruptions. Those few precious hours reminded us of what life was like pre-baby and gave us the opportunity to pretend to rejoin civilization. We would miss Allie. But stepping out allowed us to remember just how much we were blessed as a little family.

21

Limited

Things are Always Half-done

[Olive]

I've gotten really good at leaving things unfinished.

Being a mother of a young child means that most of my things to do are in a state of partially complete by the time evening rolls around. Dishes? Half in the washer, half in the sink. Emails – read but not responded to. Conversations are often interrupted and books take three times as long to get through.

Having a baby ran me headfirst into my limits. There were only 24 hours in a day and so many of those hours were necessarily spent tending to the needs of my child. I also only had so much energy. Other things had to wait or be completed piecemeal.

At first, it frustrated me that I couldn't get much done. But then I realized that my limits forced me to set priorities. I had to choose wisely and make the most of my resources. It made me evaluate what I was spending my time and energy on and made me live more intentionally.

I also learned the important lesson of counting all the small ways I had loved my family throughout the day and celebrating those accomplishments.

[Tim]

There's a comic strip circulating on the Internet about a man coming home to his wife and baby. The wife excitedly tells her husband, "I washed three dishes today! That's 50% more than what I did yesterday."

When I went back to work after my parental leave, I would come home and Olive would often complain about how much she did not get done during the day. I would be as disappointed as she was, because that usually meant that we would have to spend our evening doing dishes, laundry, or buying groceries, rather than my preferred evening activity of sitting on the couch and catching up on our favourite TV shows.

Now that I've spent many days as a stay-at-home dad this year, I understand how challenging it can be to get anything done. It's difficult trying to wash the dishes with a baby clinging to my leg or trying to fold the laundry quicker than the baby is unfolding it. The best time to get things done is when the baby is taking a nap. Unfortunately, that is also the best time for me to rest.

Even though I understand how challenging it is to get things done while taking care of Allie, I'm still disappointed when either Olive or I have not finished our to-do list for the day. But staying disappointed or complaining doesn't seem to help the situation.

What I'm learning to do is to celebrate the things that did get done. Whenever Olive laments about what she hasn't done, I ask her what she has done. Sometimes, to both of our amazement, the things that she did finish are many. She surprises even herself. And even if she only did wash three dishes the entire day, we try to celebrate that. The important thing is to remind Olive (and myself) that she is loved and worthy of love no matter how productive or unproductive she's been. This is a truth that we want Allie to know, and we want to teach her by living it out in our lives.

22

Envious

I Want to Go to Hawaii Too

[Tim]

I hate my friends - especially the ones who go to Hawaii and post half-naked photos of themselves lying on sunny beaches drinking piña coladas. I want to be in Hawaii too. Facebook should have an option for new parents to block out all the fun and interesting activities that their single friends are doing.

I am envious of my friends that do not have children. I am envious of my own life before Allie. That life was so free. I could sleep in every weekend. I could line up for midnight showings of movies. I could go snowboarding. I could go out to eat whenever I wanted. I could go travel and live spontaneously.

Now I am stuck at home with a whiny baby. What makes it worse is that it's too cold and rainy to go outside. Everywhere I go this little baby follows me and leaves a trail of havoc behind her. It feels like she constantly needs my attention. I can't even go to the washroom in peace anymore.

During these moments of envy, I stop and remind myself that Olive and I did have three years of married life without children. We made the most of that time and I'm grateful for it. Then I look at my cute baby girl. She smiles at me and melts my heart. And I decide I wouldn't trade these days for the world.

The ironic thing is that some of my single friends say that they see all the photos of me being married and with Allie and confess they are envious of my life. Maybe they are thinking that Facebook should be blocking all their married and parent friends who keep posting happy family photos online.

Perhaps everyone has "the grass is greener on the other side" syndrome, no matter where they are at in life. I like what songwriter John Charles Butler says, "The grass may be greener on the other side, but it is just as hard to mow."

[Olive]

"Comparison is the thief of joy," Theodore Roosevelt once said. I've found it to be all too true, especially after becoming a parent. It's very easy to look at my chaotic, messy, stay-at-home life now and pine for the "good old days" when things were more predictable and less complex. Or to look at someone else's children and think, "How come Allie isn't more like that?"

Of course, I never consider what my life might be like if I had twin toddlers and a newborn, like my friend does. Nor do I really know the challenges of having a child who is more like so-and-so. I only focus on the things that seem appealing to me that I don't have. I neglect to remember all the hardships I have been spared from.

I don't like who I become when I start comparing. I get all tunnel-visioned and grumpy. I cease to live in the present and stop laughing. I become enslaved to a mentality of entitlement. I forget to be grateful.

Ann Voskamp, in her excellent book, *One Thousand Gifts*, writes, "Thanks is what multiplies joy and makes any life large, and I hunger for it." So instead of comparing and envying what others have, I'm learning to look at all that I have been blessed with, give thanks and feel my joy multiply.

23

Worried

Will We Have Enough?

[Tim]

With the arrival of our baby came the new burden of having another mouth to feed. Ever since Olive was pregnant, I started worrying whether we would have enough money to provide adequate food, shelter, and opportunities for Allie.

Canadian Living estimates the cost of raising a child until the age of 18 to be $240,000.[2] Baby Center estimates the number to be $180,000[3] and the Huffington Post puts the number at $235,000 for middle-class families.[1] Those numbers scare me.

Olive usually calmly reminds me that we will make it work and everything will turn out fine. I wish I had her confidence.

The responsibility to provide for my family feels like a heavy burden. During these times I remind myself of the wise words of Jesus, "Do not worry about tomorrow, for tomorrow will worry about itself. Each day has enough trouble of its own."[5] It takes practice to leave tomorrow's worries for tomorrow and believe that our best is good enough for today.

[Olive]

Tim worries about not having enough money. I worry about not having enough energy.

When I was 27 years old, I went through a period of burn out. It took me three years before I was able to say I had fully recovered. I never returned to my "old self" though. My new normal was significantly more low key and low energy than how I had previously lived. Part of that came from having a better understanding of myself. Part of it was simply a matter of my body mellowing with age.

One of my biggest fears when I found out I was going to be a mother was that I would not have enough energy to cope with all of its demands and that I would fall into depression as a result. Well, I made it through the first year of motherhood without any major catastrophes – mostly because Tim helped and supported me.

Yet, I still worry because my low energy affects more than just our every day activities. Most weeks, I can manage to get our clothes washed and food on the table, but I fear that my lack of energy would impact the overall development of my child.

I often struggle with the question of whether Allie has enough exposure to other people. Will she grow up socially handicapped in some way because I don't have the capacity to go to all these activities and groups with her? Will she miss out on some important interpersonal skills because her mother can't handle being with people all the time?

It's easy for me to doubt whether I'm really a good mother in this way. But then I remind myself that God chose this particular child to grow up in my home, fully knowing my personality and limits. God also knows what Allie needs most and God knows what I need, too. When I think of that, my mind is a little more at ease.

24

Lonely

I Miss My Friends

[Olive]

The first year of parenthood had its fair share of lonely moments. Having a baby meant that our lives were restricted by her schedule. Sure, there were those parents who managed to go out for late nights and traipse across town every week even after their baby arrived. But we were not those parents.

Being a person with limited energy to start with, anything beyond a ten-minute drive was like a day trip for me. And if my baby wasn't sleeping well, I was the one who got stressed. I also thrived on having a regular rhythm. For most of Allie's first year, her bedtime was around 7 pm. This meant that if we wanted to go out, either only one of us could go, or we would have to find a babysitter. Evening events were hard to attend. Not to mention wake up time was always 5 am or 6 am, so as tempting as it was to stay up later for one night, we would have a price to pay the next morning.

I often found myself wishing that someone, anyone, would phone me up or at least send me a text message. I understood though that most people would hesitate to do so. After all, they wouldn't want to intrude on my "busy" day now that I had a baby to care for or unintentionally interrupt me if I was sleeping. I wanted to tell the world, "Please don't assume that I don't want to be contacted!" If I wasn't able to answer, I had voicemail. And if I really did not want to be disturbed, I could set the phone to silent.

I remember talking to a friend who had a baby shortly before I did and she told me that motherhood could sometimes feel isolating. After I had Allie, I understood just how much those little gestures of connection mattered.

[Tim]

"I miss my friends," Olive would say to me.

"At least you have friends," I half-jokingly, half-seriously replied.

Currently Olive and I both work as writers, so we work from home and don't get interaction with co-workers. When it is my turn to take care of Allie during the day, I find myself wishing I had friends to hang out with. But most of my friends and family are working during the day. All of my parent friends that don't work live too far away to visit. In the evening, I am usually too tired to want to go out and socialize.

Some days I will take Allie to a local drop-in program for babies and toddlers – either at the library, elementary school, or non-profit center. I am usually the only father there. As Allie is having the time of her life playing with new toys, I am sitting alone in the corner watching the moms chatting happily with each other. I find myself wishing I knew someone or that someone would come talk with me. I wish I had the social energy to go meet new people and make new friends, but I don't.

I feel isolated and it gets lonely. Sometimes it can be weeks without seeing anyone I know besides Olive and Allie. Don't get me wrong, I enjoy their company. But I miss my friends.

25

Confused

Baby Hallucinations

[Tim]

It was the week before Allie turned one. For some reason she hadn't been sleeping well and regularly woke up crying in the middle of the night.

At 2 am one morning, I awoke to discover Olive holding Allie, fast asleep in our bed.

"Oh no," I thought, "Allie must have been crying and Olive woke up to rock her to sleep. But Olive got so tired that she and Allie just fell asleep together in our bed."

As we had never had Allie sleep in our bed before, I decided that I'd better put Allie back in the safety of her crib so that Olive and I would not accidentally squash her.

Before I went to pick up Allie I thought I'd better lay out her blanket first so that I could more easily settle her in her crib. I got out of bed to go to Allie's room. In the dark, I reached down and felt a lump in the crib. Uh oh.

I quickly pulled my hand back but it was too late – I had woken up Allie. She lifted her head, looked at me, and started to whimper. I quickly picked her up to rock her before her whimper became a full-out cry.

I was so confused. If Allie was here, who was the baby in our bed? Did we have another baby? (I actually seriously considered this…) Who was it that I saw in our bed?

I didn't have time to go back to our room to look because I had a startled baby in my arms that I now had to calm down. Kicking myself for waking up a perfectly sleeping baby at 2 am, I started rocking Allie and walking around, trying to soothe her back to sleep.

When Allie finally drifted off again, I curiously went to our bedroom and looked in our bed to discover just Olive and no baby. I contemplated waking Olive up to ask her where the baby had gone, but I guess I was alert enough by that time to know that this was not a good idea.

I had experienced phantom rocking, when I automatically rocked back and forth even when I had no baby in my arms. I'd experienced phantom crying, when I heard the sound of a baby crying when Allie wasn't even home. But this was very different. It was like a hallucination. I saw a baby that wasn't there.

"Olive is going to laugh at me when I tell her this," I thought as I tried to go back to sleep. And she did. She thought it was the funniest thing ever. Well, at least someone was amused.

[*Olive*]

Yep. I'm still laughing.

26

Anxious

I Hope I Don't Scar My Child for Life

[Olive]

I hadn't expected it, but the prospect of introducing solid food to Allie's diet surfaced some deep anxiety in me.

Ever since I was a child, I'd had digestive problems. I love food and need to eat often, but I also have to be careful about what I eat and whether I eat frequently enough. Having spent countless hours dealing with and suffering from abdominal pain, the last thing I wanted for Allie was for her to develop the same issues.

My own mother became a holistic nutritionist a few years ago. Knowing what she knows now, she is convinced that a lot of my stomach problems could have been prevented if she had fed me differently when I was young.

So when Allie reached the six-month mark, I was very cautious.

We decided to start introducing solids with rice. After

all, we are Chinese. To our delight, she loved it! She ate it up with such glee and laughed every time she had a bite. It was so fun to feed her. We had no problem getting the food into our baby. The issue was getting it to come out the other end. I became almost paranoid about what she should or shouldn't eat.

I didn't want to be so anxious about it. It seemed like I was over-thinking things. But food and nourishment were pretty basic to life, and quite important.

Perhaps it was pressure that I put on myself. Being a first-time mom, I preferred not to screw up my child's life right from the get-go. I could envision her being a picky eater or having food issues in the future… "It's all because you fed me rice and not avocado!" She would blame me. In reality, that will probably not be the case. Still, it was hard for me not to let my fears get the best of me.

Food is meant to be enjoyed. That's what I remind myself these days. Hopefully, she will grow up with positive associations with food. Hopefully, my issues won't pass on to her. But even if they do, it'll be part of her humanness.

[Tim]

Initially I felt excited to start feeding Allie solid foods. It was so much fun watching her reactions to new tastes (everything probably tasted delicious after a strict six month diet of only breast milk, which tastes shockingly bland and a bit bitter – yes, I did try some).

Olive took on the main responsibility of deciding what to feed Allie, which was why I probably didn't feel as anxious as she did. Basically whatever Olive prepared, I would feed

Allie. And if Allie didn't like it, I would report back to Olive and let her decide what to do next.

Sometimes I could see that Olive's worry about food was getting overwhelming and I would try to reassure her that things would be okay. Other times my wife's worries would be infectious, and we would both sit there discussing what to do.

"What if it's the applesauce that's causing Allie to be constipated?" Olive would ask me.

"Uh. I've never thought of that." I would respond while sarcastically thinking, "Thanks for introducing me to a new reason to worry." Anxiety can be contagious.

27

Enlivened

The Most Beautiful Sound

[Tim]

I still remember the first time Allie laughed. It was pure music to my ears and the most beautiful thing I'd ever heard in my life. Ever since that day, I became addicted to Allie's little laugh. I can't get enough of it.

My life is like a video game where I score points every time I get Allie to laugh – that's my goal for the entire day. But it's totally random what makes her laugh. So I try everything. I make silly faces, I play peek-a-boo, I hide behind the door and jump out to surprise her. I tickle her or chase her around. And when I do find that funny something that gets her to laugh, I feel immense satisfaction. She laughs and I laugh and Olive laughs and it is pure joy.

Babies seem to laugh so much, but for some reason as we grow older we seem to laugh less and less. Are things less funny? Or have we gotten too serious? I think the reason people love babies and children is because they laugh so much. Their laughter is infectious and makes everyone happy. William Thackeray said, "A good laugh is sunshine in the house." My baby's laugh is sunshine in my life.

[Olive]

There are very few things in this world that I think should be mandatory for everyone. Daily baby laughter therapy is one of them. It's literally impossible not to feel my spirit lift when I hear the sound of my baby laughing. Any baby's laughter makes me smile, but Allie's laughter is particularly sweet to my ears.

Of the two of us, Tim is better at making Allie laugh. Maybe it's because he's ~~funnier looking~~ the bigger goof. I sometimes envy the ease at which he can elicit her giggles. When I'm with Allie and I happen to make her laugh, I feel like I've hit the jackpot.

When my child laughs, I think, "Yes! This is why I love being a parent!" Her laughter makes all the hard work and sleepless nights worth it.

Tim and I are not the only ones who love to hear Allie laugh. One of my best friends wants to record it for her ringtone.

Tim says Allie's laugh is like sunshine in his life. To me, her laugh is a little touch of heaven.

The Ride
As a Couple

28

Exhuasted

Wake Up! It's 2 am!

[Tim]

Those first few weeks after Alena was born, Olive and I attempted to work out a schedule that allowed both of us to get as much sleep as possible while caring for Allie. We were grateful that I could take parental leave from work so I could be home full time.

I tried to let Olive rest as much as possible so that she could focus on recovering from labour and figuring out the breast pumping thing. So those first few weeks after Allie was born, I did the majority of diaper changing and feeding.

This was our typical evening/night schedule:

8 pm: Olive pump and eat

8:30 pm: Tim feed, change, bathe, rock Allie to sleep

9 pm: Olive sleep

11 pm: Tim feed, change, rock Allie to sleep, Tim sleep

Midnight: Olive pump, eat, and sleep

2 am: Tim feed, change, rock Allie to sleep, Tim sleep
4 am: Olive pump, eat, and sleep
5:30 am: Tim feed, change, rock Allie to sleep, Tim sleep
8 am: Olive pump, eat, and sleep

The hardest thing to do was wake up at 2 am to feed Allie. I would hear her cry, but it was so, so, so difficult to get up. 2 am was smack in the middle of the deepest part of my sleep cycle.

After Allie cried for who knows how long, I would finally drag my tired body out of bed and stumble into Allie's room to pick her up and calm her. Still half-asleep, I would warm up her milk and feed her. Then I would change her and rock her back to sleep. The key was to try to do all this before I had fully woken up, so I could go back to bed and hopefully fall asleep quickly.

Every night looked a bit different. We wrote down everything that happened on a spreadsheet on our fridge. This allowed us to get a better sense of Allie's rhythms. During those first few months Olive and I did our best to work together to figure out the optimal arrangement to care for Allie while caring for each other.

[Olive]

Toward the end of my pregnancy, I would get up periodically at night to pee and sometimes, to eat. We would joke about how my body was simply getting me ready for when the baby was born. We laughed about it, but it was also true.

Tim didn't get the same preparation so waking up at 2

am was harder on him. Not that it was any easier for me to wake up in the middle of the night. There were definitely times when I felt a bit resentful that I could not sleep to my heart's content. But I also had to remind myself not to feel guilty about staying in bed when Tim took the 2 am feeding.

Those first couple of months really felt like one long endless night punctuated by feedings with little naps in between. I was thankful that Tim could be home and that he was willing to take on more of the load so that I could recover. We were both pretty much hanging by a thread and it helped to know that we could tag team our efforts.

The initial weeks felt endlessly exhausting. But it helped to know we could work together and support each other through it.

29

Forgotten

Does Anyone Remember Me?

[Tim]

Allie was about 8 weeks old and both sets of our parents had come and gone. Christmas was also over. It was just Olive, the baby, and me. But most of the time, it just felt like the baby and me.

I found myself spending more and more time watching TV or surfing the Internet. I would put Allie to bed and stay up watching TV shows or Youtube videos for hours, even though I was dead tired. Then I would feel guilty afterwards for wasting time and not sleeping. And I would feel extra tired the next morning. This lasted for a few weeks.

One thing I'd learned over the years was that beating myself up and wallowing in my guilt for lack of self-control was not constructive. So instead, I extended grace to myself and started reflecting about why this was happening.

What I started realizing was that TV was an escape from

reality. It was something I did to indulge myself, and it made me feel happy temporarily because it was something I could do that was solely for myself. I realized I was especially craving attention at that time because I felt forgotten.

Olive was constantly tired and still recovering from her labour. She was so absorbed with taking care of herself and the baby that I felt like she had completely forgotten about me.

On top of that, I hadn't had a real conversation with a friend in a long time. Everyone that came to visit was too busy cooing over the baby and asking Olive about her labour or breastfeeding. I felt like a spectator.

One evening, my siblings were able to come over and watch Allie so Olive and I could go on a short date. We picked up some drinks and donuts from a nearby coffee shop, drove to a scenic point by our house, stopped the car and just talked.

It was a rare moment for us to be together, just the two of us, without having to worry about the baby.

"How are you doing?" Olive asked me.

I knew Olive probably had no idea how I was really feeling. I hadn't wanted to burden her with anything extra. But I knew that in a way, by not telling her, I was being selfish. By keeping quiet, I was hiding what I was going through and not allowing Olive into that part of my life. I didn't want to seem weak and needy. But if I couldn't tell my wife, then whom could I tell? I knew that if I didn't say something, I might turn bitter towards Olive, and that was the last thing that I wanted.

"I feel... forgotten." I said slowly. The words came out

shaky. I was surprised how emotional I felt.

I started sharing with Olive. She sat and listened. When I was done, she was silent. I could tell that she was letting my words sink in.

"I'm sorry," she said. "I've been neglecting you. I know I'm tired, but I haven't left any energy for you, and that's wrong of me. Thank you for telling me this."

Dr. James Houston said, "Friendship is built on the mutual sharing of weakness." A marriage is also built on the mutual sharing of weakness. For this to be possible, our marriage needed to be a safe place where we could be vulnerable.

Looking back, that conversation was a milestone for our marriage. I felt heard and remembered. And somehow, after that conversation, the urge to indulge in hours of late-night TV lifted. I guess the affection of a real person was what I was really needing and looking for.

[Olive]

I felt bad that sex wasn't happening. I knew it was important to our marriage but it was just hard to be physically intimate when everything hurt and milk was leaking everywhere. I would hope and pray that Tim would be okay with the dry spell.

I lived in an alternate universe for the first two months after Alena was born. My world was mainly inhabited by pain and fatigue. I was pretty much consumed with simply surviving and waiting for my body to recover. I knew Tim was there and I was deeply grateful that he could take up the bulk of caring for Allie, but I had excruciatingly little to give to him.

At the back of my mind, I knew that I probably needed to give him more attention, but he seemed to be getting by. It wasn't until our conversation in the car that I realized he needed more than my physical love. He needed me to be mindful of him, to acknowledge him and to express my appreciation for him.

Looking back, those months were a hazy blur. I think it's a gift of grace that Tim didn't become bitter or resentful of me during that time. And I'm really thankful that we had that hour to talk.

30

Angry

Whose Side Are You On?

[Olive]

I'm generally an easy-going, cheerful type of person but there was one night when I felt like my inner monster reared its ferocious head. It was supposed to be a happy night. My in-laws and Tim's brother were visiting from Asia. Everyone was thrilled to play with Allie. They were only visiting for a short time so we wanted to let them spend as much time as possible with her.

That evening, everyone came over for dinner. After dinner, I knew that we needed to put Allie to bed. She had already been showing signs of tiredness as we had been eating. Tim thought it would be okay to let her stay up a little later than usual, seeing as it was a rare occasion that the whole family was together. Not wanting to disappoint the family, I let her continue playing.

I knew that Allie had a window of tiredness when she

would be able to fall asleep quickly but after that window passed, she would be over-stimulated and getting her to sleep would be more difficult. I suspected that we might have to pay for it later, but I convinced myself that we would be able to handle it.

Eventually, everyone left and we started Allie on her bedtime routine. By then, it was already a couple hours past her usual bedtime. Not surprisingly, she started crying and resisting sleep. I tried to rock her to calm her.

Two hours later of breaking my back trying to calm and settle her, she was still wailing and refusing to sleep. I was furious.

It felt like a battle of wills.

I was angry because she was being her own worst enemy. I was angry because I could have potentially prevented this from happening. I was internally scolding myself for going against my better judgment, for not insisting on putting her to bed earlier and for letting our relatives keep stimulating her with their tablet and smartphone screens. I was upset that they could all happily go to sleep while we had to stay up, paying the price for their entertainment.

I felt like I was at the end of my rope; that if I continued holding her, I would hurt her in some way. So I put her in her crib, shut the door on her cries and walked into our room where Tim was reading in bed. Seething with emotion, I picked up the nearest pillow and slammed it down hard on the mattress. And then I added my tears to Allie's wails.

Tim graciously (and perhaps cautiously) offered to try to put Allie to sleep so that I could have a break and decompress. Exhausted as I was, I couldn't sleep. I turned to my journal.

Writing it out allowed me to figure out the real cause of my anger. In the heat of the moment, I had only known what I felt angry about – I hadn't understood why. But as I had time to work through my emotions and thoughts, I realized that I had been upset because I felt like Tim hadn't listened to me. He had seemed to put appeasing his family above wanting what was best for Allie.

Allie eventually fell asleep, but not before it was midnight. Tim and I had a good talk afterwards about what really happened.

[Tim]

Olive isn't a person who gets angry easily, so I am usually surprised to see her angry. That night she was the angriest I've ever seen her.

I had really wanted my family to enjoy Allie's company so I'd glossed over Olive's concerns and told her that letting our baby stay up would be okay. Allie seemed super energetic and a bit hyper as well, which made her extra hilarious and entertaining for everyone. Olive wasn't happy, but she let me have my way.

When it became clear that it might be a long night ahead, we decided to take turns trying to get Allie to sleep while the other got ready for bed.

I went to take a shower first and told Olive to come get me when she got tired. After my shower, I sat in our bed reading and waiting for my turn.

It was around 11:30 pm when Olive all of a sudden stormed in. She picked up her pillow and slammed it on the bed, forcefully blurting out, "I'm so angry!" Then she started crying.

I was startled. When my wife gets angry, I'm not exactly sure what to do. What I want to do is tell her not to be angry because anger is an emotion that makes me uncomfortable. But that's probably the worst thing you could say to a person that feels angry.

Part of me started to feel guilty because I wondered if she was angry with me. My mind started racing and thinking about all the possible things I did that could have made her angry. Maybe she was angry about something else, I hoped. But there was still this lingering feeling that I was in trouble.

I told Olive to take a break. I would take over and try to get Allie to sleep. I rocked the baby until I got too tired to carry her, then I put her in the crib. After 10-15 minutes of crying, she finally fell asleep.

I went back to our room and Olive was journaling. As an internal processor, my wife needed her own space to work out her emotions and thoughts first. So I told her that I loved her, reassured her that she was a good mom and was doing a good job, and went to sleep.

The next day we talked about the incident. Part of me dreaded the conversation because I sensed that somehow I did something wrong, and I don't like making mistakes and having anyone be angry with me. But I knew that growing our marriage meant that we needed to have these hard conversations and work through the conflict.

Olive shared her point of view with me. She felt like I had not supported her, that I had taken my family's side over her side the previous evening. It wasn't so much about the decision to let Allie stay up, but the process of making the decision, where Olive felt like it was my family and my wishes against hers.

It was helpful to understand Olive's perspective, how she felt and why she felt that way. I would have felt the same if I were in her shoes. In our marriage we had promised each other that we would be on the same team, and that evening I had broken that promise. I apologized to Olive, she graciously forgave me, and our marriage moved one step forward instead of one step back.

Reflecting back, I realized this: One of the challenging things in our marriage is building the relationship with our in-laws. When I take my family's side over my wife's side (whether it be in following their preferences or their traditions), I make things worse because it makes Olive feel like she is competing with my family for my attention. That does not help their relationship. But if I always take Olive's side, then she will not feel threatened by my family. Taking Olive's side does not mean I do whatever she wants, but that I consider her opinion first and foremost, and work with her to make a decision together. It's a tricky thing, and having a baby is giving us many chances to learn and re-learn it.

31

Conflicted

When We Don't Agree with Each Other

[Olive]

After the first few months of Alena's life, we thought we were doing great. I was pumping more than enough milk. She was wetting and pooping like a champ. She was strong, growing and healthy. We finally felt like we were getting the hang of this raising a baby thing.

Then came teeth. And solid foods. And constipation.

And differences of opinion.

In terms of healthcare, Tim and I had very different views. He trusted the Western medical system and I believed more in natural methods of treatment. We were both skeptical of each other's preferences. This wasn't surprising, considering his mother used to be a pharmacist and my mother is currently a holistic nutritionist. It's what we've grown up with.

Before we had a child, our differences in this area didn't

affect us that much. We each just did our own thing. I would go to the chiropractor and take vitamins while Tim would go to the doctor and take medicine. Now that we had Alena, we had to actually address our differences.

Our child was obviously in distress. She would cry in pain every time she tried to pass a stool. It hurt her, but it also hurt us to see her in that condition. We needed to do something. But what?

Tim's cousin was a pediatrician. We asked him about Allie's situation and he gave us a recommendation for a safe over-the-counter laxative we could administer to her. He reassured us that constipation was completely normal for babies and young children, and told us that if it was treated early, it wouldn't have damaging effects on our child.

We also asked my mom. She suggested prune juice, more water during the day, a daily consistent "poop time," and giving Allie baby probiotics.

I realized that it was one thing to have preference about treatment options, but it was quite another thing when your child was in pain. The holistic approach usually took a while to have an effect and we knew Allie needed quicker help. So despite my hesitations, we gave her the laxative first. Within a day, we saw improvement. Never did I think I would be so glad to see another person poop!

Tim and I revisited the conversation often, tracking Allie's progress and coming up with next steps together. Eventually, we took her off of the laxative and implemented my mom's suggestions.

We still don't have the same views on healthcare and we will likely bump up against other parenting differences in the future, but this experience gave us an opportunity to practice hearing each other out and being open to the other's way of doing things.

[Tim]

What happens when parents disagree on how to raise their children and what's best for them? How do they decide what to do?

Many things Olive and I agreed on, but there was one thing we seemed to fight about all the time – it came down to how to approach Allie's health.

Olive wanted Allie to take probiotics.

I wanted Allie to take laxatives.

She wanted to use cloth diapers.

I wanted to use disposable diapers.

She preferred feeding Allie homemade purées.

I just bought jars of baby food at the grocery store.

Sometimes I felt like whoever was more stubborn would get their way. It felt good to be right, so we both tried hard to win.

The hard part about fighting and having conflict as new parents was that we rarely had the energy or time to resolve the conflict. It seemed like we would have the same type of fight over and over again.

Psychologist and marriage counselor Robert C. Dodds said, "The goal of marriage is not to think alike, but to think together." In being parents and having the responsibility of taking care of another individual, we had to learn how to think together. We had to learn how to work as a team and not insist on doing things our way (a.k.a. "the right way"). We had to learn how to appreciate each other's perspective, and treat each other with respect. And we had to learn how to make decisions together, even on issues we did not agree upon.

This may be the most difficult thing about parenting. We have the choice either to let our fights and disagreements pull our marriage apart, or use these circumstances to grow our marriage.

Regarding Allie's health, I let Olive make the decisions in the end. She was more knowledgeable in this area and more interested in doing the research on the pros and cons of different treatments. What I wanted and hoped for was that in making her decision, she would listen and seriously consider my point of view first. What I had to learn was to empower her to make the decision and to fully support her in it, even if I disagreed. We were a team and needed to work together and support each other.

32

Guilty

I Dropped My Baby (Again)

[Tim]

It's amazing how quickly Allie forgot her pain and forgave me. I wasn't so quick to forgive myself. In fact, I felt like a complete failure of a dad. It was easily my worst day as a father.

It was a Saturday in early July, shortly after we had moved into our new home. I was trying to multi-task by watching Allie and doing some housework at the same time. I put Allie in the middle of our bed while I unpacked a box of books. She had just learned how to roll over, but did not roll very often – it felt safe to place her there for a minute.

As I happily unpacked a box, feeling proud of myself for being so productive, I suddenly heard a loud thud behind me. There was the slightest moment of silence before the cry came. I'll never forget the sharp and piercing cry that came from my baby.

I rushed over to pick up my wailing daughter from the floor. Tears were streaming down her little chubby cheeks. I held her but she was inconsolable. Then Olive rushed into the room.

"What happened??" she asked me.

"She fell off the bed," I answered sheepishly. Olive gave me a fierce look that said, "How could you let this happen to our only daughter?" She quickly took the crying Allie from my arms and whisked her away from her dangerous and reckless father.

I was left standing there. Alone, shocked and feeling guilty. Very guilty. The guilt felt like a heavy knot in my stomach mixed with a sour taste in the back of my mouth. My head felt dizzy and my throat felt tight.

I felt like a failure.

I had failed as a father. Failed in protecting my daughter. Failed at keeping her safe. That was my job. It was so simple. But no, I had to do my own thing and try to be productive.

When I told the story to my friends, they reassured me that I wasn't the first parent to drop his baby. I also knew this would not be the only time I would make a mistake as a parent and hurt Allie. (It wasn't. A few months later I dropped her again, but even worse. This time it left a small scar on her face.)

Making mistakes as a new father gives me opportunities to practice responding to guilt. I could beat myself up and carry this guilt around, or I could choose to forgive myself. And I want to be able to forgive myself and live free from guilt.

Failures are part of life and opportunities to learn rich

lessons. But if my value and worth are tied to performing and achieving, then it makes it difficult to face failures. We want Allie to know that she is valued and worthy of love no matter if she succeeds or fails. If she can believe this, then she will be able to face and embrace the failures in her life.

A possible upside is when Allie does something stupid later on in life and a friend snidely asks her, "Were you dropped on your head as a baby?" Allie can honestly respond, "Yes, twice." And refer to this chapter as proof.

[Olive]

The first time Tim dropped Alena, I was shocked and mad. I quickly ran into the room and whisked my crying baby out of his arms and tried to calm her by taking her outdoors. I wanted to save her from her inattentive dad.

Then Tim blogged about how devastated he was when I took her away and I realized I had caused him more grief by doing what I did. Allie was resilient and she most likely wouldn't remember falling. Tim, however, needed reassurance that mistakes were okay in our home.

The second time he dropped her, I knew to respond differently. (Sorry, Allie, for letting you fall so many times!) I bit my tongue and willed myself to keep washing the dishes, even though both my husband and daughter were distraught. I knew that I had to give them time to process what had happened and to mend their relationship before it was appropriate for me to step in.

Naturally, I had some unkind thoughts toward Tim in that moment, but I knew he didn't need me to pile on any more guilt than he was already feeling so I kept my thoughts to myself. I also needed some time to calm down – to remind myself that Allie was fine and that it could have happened on my watch as well.

I needed to extend compassion to Tim, to forgive him and to give him another chance. After all, we were both learning to be parents. And if the tables were turned and I was the guilty party, I would want that grace, too.

It wasn't easy to forgive my husband for dropping my precious baby. But for the sake of all three of us, it was the necessary and important decision to make.

33

Sad

Weaning

[Olive]

I made it my "breastfeeding goal" to nurse Allie until she was a year old. After that, I reasoned, her system could probably handle transitioning to other milk.

As her birthday approached, I felt amazed that I had been able to pump enough milk for her entire first year of life. Tim started hinting to me that I could probably pump less and slowly decrease my output. (The body produces milk based on the demand; so less output meant less production.) My head knew that was the reasonable thing to do. But my heart had a much harder time being okay with the transition.

Feeding Allie milk from my body was the one and only thing that I could exclusively do for her – well, aside from being her mother. For all her other needs, others could take my place. But providing her milk that had been produced by me was the last tie I had to the days before she was born, when she was completely dependent on me for everything. The irony, of course, was that less than a year ago, I had wanted to escape this responsibility. Even now, part of me wanted to be done with it. But as I faced the reality of this transition, it felt like a loss of sorts.

Weaning was really the first of many steps toward her independence:

Soon she would be walking, and not need me to carry her.

Then she would be going to school and making her own friends, and not need me to play with her.

Then she would learn to cook and not need me to feed her.

And one day, she would move out and not need me to take care of her.

I was happy she was growing up. But I was also sad.

[Tim]

I was actually hoping that Olive would start weaning earlier. The breast pumping was a hassle, with all the bottles to wash, the bags of extra milk taking up space in the freezer, and having to plan our day around Olive's pumping schedule. Plus, I was eager for Allie to graduate to the next level of drinking cow's milk.

When Olive insisted that she breastfeed until the one-year mark (and maybe beyond), I was slightly annoyed. She obviously did not care that her breast pumping complicated our lives – because if she did, then she would not be disagreeing with me.

In most cases when Olive feels strongly about something, there usually is a deeper reason. During another one of our discussions about transitioning Allie to regular milk, Olive shared with me this sadness she felt about stopping breastfeeding. I had this "Aha" moment and finally understood why Olive was resisting my very logical plan of weaning Allie.

It was helpful to understand Olive's point of view. Now that I could empathize with her, I knew it wasn't the best idea to keep pushing her to stop breastfeeding. And because I understood, I was able to give her the space and time she needed, while encouraging her that she would always have a special and important place in Allie's life, even if she wasn't Allie's milk factory anymore.

Marriage authors Drs. Les and Leslie Parrot say that 90% of conflict in marriage is resolved if the couple can empathize with each other and see the other's point of view. From our experience, this seems to be true.

34

Content

Reviewing the Day's Highlights

[Tim]

At the end of the day, when Olive and I are lying in bed, we usually have some time to chat. It's one of our favourite moments each day. Too often we find that the day goes by rather quickly and although we may have seen each other several times, we might not have actually connected.

After becoming parents, I noticed that many of our favourite moments from each day included Allie.

"It was so cute when Allie learned to put up both hands and say 'Mmmm?'" I would imitate her, and we would look at each other and laugh.

"It's so funny when Allie complains by saying 'Wa-wa-wa-wa-wa!'"

"Allie looked so delighted with herself for being able to clap her hands."

Sometimes we would watch videos or photos of Allie that we had taken during the day.

However, these moments aren't always in the evening. Whenever one of us spends time with Alena alone (while the other is working, sleeping or out), we will recap the highlights to the other person and tell them what they missed.

Remembering those moments makes me feel content and especially grateful that I have my wife Olive to share the wonder, mayhem, and hilarity of parenthood with. In a way, learning to be parents together has deepened our relationship with each other.

[Olive]

The bulk of being a parent to a young child is mundane, tiring and boring work. When we recount our experiences with Allie during the day, we are reminded of why it's all worth it. Her developments and successes are our developments and successes. Her enjoyment of life makes us enjoy life more. When we celebrate our daughter, we are brought closer as a couple.

We struggle, we worry, we fret, but in the midst of it, Allie reminds us to smile, to laugh and to remember how blessed we are to be able to witness her growth together.

The Ride As
Friends and Family

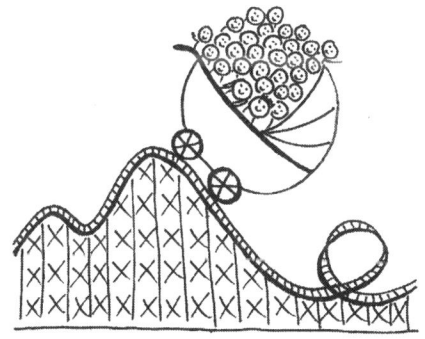

35

Overjoyed

Sharing Our Baby with Loved Ones

[Tim]

After we got pregnant, I had a blast sharing the exciting news with our friends and family. From cooking a baby-themed dinner for my family (i.e. baby-back ribs, baby carrots, and baby bok choy) to creating a "Future Canucks Fan" t-shirt with an arrow pointing to Olive's belly and posting it on Facebook, I loved sharing our joy with our loved ones.

As much as I loved telling people we were expecting, I was overjoyed to actually introduce them to Allie – especially my family. From the first time our parents and siblings held Allie at the hospital to their visits throughout the first year, I loved watching them interact with baby Allie.

Whenever they came to visit, I tried to give them the full

baby experience. Whatever chance I got, I asked if they wanted to feed Allie, change her diapers, or rock her to sleep. Our siblings, Dan, Tiff and Simon, did almost anything. My parents and Olive's parents were selective and stayed away from changing diapers. "We've changed our fair share of dirty diapers," was their excuse.

I loved watching my family as they carefully held Allie and put the bottle to her mouth. I would slowly instruct them and encourage them. When Allie would start feeding, I loved watching the sense of satisfaction, joy, and accomplishment on their faces.

Three weeks after Allie was born, the entire family celebrated Christmas together. Olive's parents were visiting from Toronto and my parents had just flown in from Hong Kong. Together with Dan, Tiff, and Simon, we all gathered for a delicious dinner and exchanged gifts in our apartment. Everyone was fighting for their turn to hold Allie.

Both Olive and I feel like having a baby has deepened our relationships with our family, especially with the family that we each married into. It was an unexpected gift that we felt very fortunate about. Yes the baby did cause some rifts and strain in our relationships, but we worked through those. I think it was because we now all had a common person to dote on and to love.

Allie was a way through which I could get to know my in-laws better, and through which Olive got to know my parents and siblings better too. Because of Allie, stories from Olive's and my childhood would surface, and we would feel more connected to each other's families as a result.

Before the baby came, our parents would visit us about once a year. During Allie's first year, my in-laws doubled their visits and my parents tripled their visits. We were happy to see them more often. Who knows? Maybe with a few more grandchildren they might end up moving here!

[Olive]

With Alena's arrival, it was like we were given a tiny, mesmerizing and joy-inducing gift that we got to share with the world. Our baby was her own person, for sure, but she was also a part of us. Her presence gave us another valuable point of connection with the people in our lives.

I will never forget the tears of joy in my friend's eyes the moment I told her I was pregnant. We were having Japanese ramen and she jumped out of her seat and raced around the table to give me a huge hug. I hadn't expected that news of my child would touch her so deeply.

It's fun, too, to watch my close friends interact with Allie. It brings me joy to see them play with her and to watch her warm up to them. Still, part of me misses having the deep conversations like we had pre-baby. Maybe I still need to get used to sharing their attention.

36

Hurt

Fighting With Our Parents

[Tim]

Before Allie was one week old, I had a big fight with Olive's parents. They were so angry they wanted to cancel Christmas.

Well, technically no one could cancel Christmas. But they wanted to cancel Christmas with us by changing their plane tickets to fly back to Toronto early.

It all started when Olive complained to me that she was tired of having our small apartment full of all these people all day long. When she said "all these people," she mostly meant her parents.

Ben and Bernadette had taken 4 weeks off and flown to Vancouver to help take care of their first grandchild, their only daughter Olive, and myself. They had been coming over every day to cook us lunch and dinner, and to help with Allie (including washing and folding the endless amount of baby laundry and doing all the dishes). But we lived in a small apartment. And Olive was highly introverted, which meant that being with people for long periods of time tired her out.

So the superhero in me came out to protect my wife. While Olive was napping one afternoon, I pulled her parents aside and had a little chat with them.

I cut right to the chase, "We need more space. Can you come over less?"

"When we leave, you're going to have to learn to take care of your family," my father-in-law informed me.

"Don't worry," I replied slightly offended, "We have friends and family who can help us too."

It seemed like they got the message because after dinner that night they quickly packed up and returned to the place they were renting. Olive and I sighed with relief, glad to have the apartment to ourselves for the evening.

I knew something was wrong when I received a text the next day from Olive's mom: "We'll come this afternoon to cook for Olive and then leave."

Ummm… cook for Olive? What about me? And sure enough, they came and cooked food for only Olive. Then they promptly left.

We didn't see them for the next two days, which was weird, because they had been coming over every day since Allie was born.

Then we received an email from Olive's dad, saying that they felt like they weren't needed and were going to fly home on December 21st, two weeks earlier than planned.

Olive and I were upset and confused. It felt like they were being unnecessarily petty. We needed their support

121

now, and yet it felt like they were just adding to our stress. It took every ounce of self-discipline not to reply with a biting email and to ask if we could have a conversation together before they made their final decision to leave early.

Olive and I called our trusted friends to vent. We knew that we needed to feel heard and listened to. If we felt heard by our friends, when we talked with Olive's parents, it would be okay if we didn't feel heard by them. We could focus on listening and hearing them out.

The day we planned to have our talk, Allie thankfully went to sleep after dinner. We had a long talk. Our conversation was very civil and revealing, as each of us was able to explain how we felt. I was glad none of us were yellers.

What I said was that we needed more space.

What my in-laws heard was that we didn't need their help.

They felt hurt, because they had been really looking forward to coming to help take care of Olive, Allie, and myself. What I said made them feel unwanted.

What they said was that I would have to learn to take care of Olive and Allie after they left.

What I heard was that they didn't think I could take care of my family.

I felt hurt because I was trying very hard to be a good father and husband. What they said made me feel like a failure.

No wonder we were angry at each other.

It helped to hear their perspective and for them to hear ours. We apologized to each other and hugged. They decided to stay for Christmas after all. Everyone was relieved.

Allie was an angel and slept through our entire conversation. Right when we finished hugging, as if on cue, she woke up. It was like she knew that everything was okay and that we could all return to our main duty of caring for her.

[Olive]

The in-law relationship starts off as a delicate creature. My parents didn't get to grow up with Tim and Tim didn't get to grow up with my parents. So it made sense that their relationship would be tested when it was placed in the sleep-deprived, high adaptation environment of our baby's first week of life.

Just because it made sense, however, it didn't make it feel any better. Their misunderstanding was the cause for more of my tears that week than the physical pain of my recovery was.

I felt caught in the middle, like somehow I had caused this. I knew both parties wanted my best and were trying their best to take care of Alena and me. But in doing so, they had clashed.

I hated conflict, particularly when it was with people who were closest to me. I just wanted everybody to get along. However, I also knew that the best way to deal with conflict was to work through it. So I mustered up what energy and strength I had, prayed for grace and arranged a conversation for the four of us.

I was thankful that my parents valued growth. I think the four of us understood that this situation was an opportunity for our relationships with each other to grow if we let it be such. Because they valued growth, they were open to trying to resolve the conflict, to listening to us and to speaking what was on their hearts.

It turned out to be an illuminating conversation; one that deepened and solidified our love and commitment to each other as family.

The timing of it all felt pretty crummy though. It was an added layer of complication to an already demanding week of adjustment. But I suppose it was as good a time for conflict as any. In a way, having newborn Allie there gave us more reason to work through it. And more grace with which to do it.

(Note: We have to thank Ben and Bernadette for allowing us to share this vulnerable story in our book.)

37

Amused

Baby Potty Humour

[Olive]

Babies are funny. They don't realize how funny they are. Maybe that's part of why they make us laugh. Much of baby humour has to do with what comes out of them. Somehow, we find it funny. Perhaps laughter is the best way to cope with the mess.

In the wee hours of the morning four days into Allie's life, we realized we needed to supplement her with some formula. We'd been warned that formula poop smelled a lot worse than breast milk poop. Little did we know the implications of our decision.

That afternoon, I awoke from my nap to my husband's alarmed voice, "Eeeeew!!! ALLLIIEEEE!!! How are you so STINKYYYYYYY?!?!?!" I emerged from our room to witness him running in circles around the baby change table while pinching his nose shut with one hand and frantically beating the air with his other hand. I immediately did what any caring wife and mother would do. I grabbed my phone and switched on the video camera function. This footage was too precious to be wasted. As I stood there filming him, hands shaking from laughter, he glared at me. I'll never forget that moment – it was just so fun laughing at Tim's expense. I only wish I'd left the video on for longer.

[Tim]

The time Allie peed on my brother was hilarity at its best.

I was giving my brother free parenting lessons: valuable, hands-on experience on bathing a 1-month old baby. (Dan, you'll thank me for having taught you this when you become a father.) I showed Dan how to hold Allie with one arm while soaping the baby with the other arm. As Dan was holding Allie, she suddenly started peeing all over his shirt. My brother gave a yelp of surprise but didn't know what to do. I would have helped but I was too busy laughing until my sides hurt.

Not wanting to play favourites, I gave my brother-in-law, Simon, the same free parenting lessons (secretly hoping Allie might pee on him too, so I could have another laugh). Allie did not disappoint. The funny thing was that Simon was so concentrated on washing Allie that he did not even notice until he felt that his feet were wet.

It was all highly amusing until I got peed on. I felt the wetness and yelled out in surprise. But my yell startled Allie and she started crying. I stood there in shock with baby pee all over my shirt and pants while holding a crying baby.

My father and my father-in-law got peed on too.

Somehow the female members of the family were spared. That first month we joked that we should form an exclusive APOM club (a.k.a. The Allie-Peed-On-Me club.) We could even have t-shirts.

38

Indignant

Unsolicited Advice

[Olive]

Before I had Alena, I would see embarrassed mothers at the checkout line trying to hold it together while their snot-faced children would be wriggling on the floor and yelling at the top of their lungs. Deep inside, I would wonder, "Why can't she control her kids?" I hoped that my own kids would be better behaved when the day came.

After becoming a mother, I quickly realized that it was difficult for me to judge another parent again. Parenting is just so complex; life is just so complex that it's impossible for me to know someone else's whole story. I simply cannot make a judgment on someone else's choices because I haven't seen the whole picture.

After all, what did I know? Their child might have a medical condition, or they might be dealing with a family crisis, or maybe they'd all had a really rough night the night before. There's just a lot more than meets the eye.

It makes me feel rather indignant when people come up to me and offer me unsolicited advice about my child. I've had people tell me it's too bright outside for my baby, that she needs to wear shoes (she didn't even know how to walk and I was wearing her in a carrier), and that I shouldn't clip her hair up.

I realize that most people offer advice because they care to some degree and want to help. But it irks me when I haven't asked for it and the other party obviously does not know my whole situation.

When someone comes up to me and tells me I should shave my baby's head so that her hair can grow thicker, this is what I hear, "You're not doing a good enough job as her mother." They may not mean for that to happen, but what unsolicited advice does is surface my own insecurities.

As a new parent, what I need most is affirmation. I have enough voices in my head pointing out ways that I fail. I definitely have a lot to learn, but I am giving it my best. Unless I'm unconsciously harming my baby, a word of encouragement will do just fine. Especially if you don't really know me.

[Tim]

Olive makes it a habit to share with me all the unsolicited parenting advice she gets. I usually laugh because some of the suggestions are so ridiculous. And I secretly feel glad because these stories provide me some amusement.

Then I receive some unsolicited advice for myself, and I start feeling indignant. "Who do you think you are to tell me that my newborn baby needs to wear clothes? She's a hot baby and is perfectly fine in just a diaper and a blanket. Plus, our apartment is very warm. What do you know about parenting anyways?" I fume to myself. Oh wait, that's my mom who gave me that advice and she's raised three kids... maybe I should actually pay attention rather than instantly dismiss her advice.

It's difficult to receive parenting advice well, especially as a first-time parent. Every time someone gives me advice I hear, "You're doing it all wrong! You're a bad parent! You're going to irreversibly and permanently damage your baby unless you change your wicked ways!" And that's not what they're saying... at least not out loud anyways.

First-time parents like myself need encouragement from others, not judgment. We need people to reassure us that we're all right and that we're doing a good job. We need someone to pat us on the back and give us a gold star, or at least a participation ribbon.

However, I am starting to learn to appreciate the unsolicited parenting advice I get. I do this by assuming that the person is taking initiative to give me advice because they care about my baby and me. When my aunt tells me, "Don't put a hairclip in your baby's hair, it will pull out all her hair and she will be bald," I try not to reply sarcastically, "Like you?" Instead I say, "Good idea. I've never thought of that before." And I say it like I mean it even though she tells me every time she sees me.

And when my Grandma calls me to tell me not to feed Allie strawberries because of something she heard on the radio, I say, "Thank you grandma." And I am actually genuinely grateful that my 91-year-old grandma is thinking about us. Besides, no one calls me these days other than telemarketers.

39

Disappointed

Why Can't She Make a Good Impression?

[Tim]

Allie was four months old and it was the first time I was taking her out on my own. Olive was too tired to go to my friend's birthday party, but I wanted to go. Many of my friends would be there and I was eager for them to meet Allie for the first time.

I was nervous about driving to the party alone, and I hoped the baby wouldn't cry all the way. The car ride there was surprisingly fine. I was one of the first to arrive. My friends were so happy to see Allie and she was doing great... at first. Then she started crying. I tried to soothe Allie but she kept crying. Thinking she might be hungry, I started feeding her some milk. She drank half the bottle and then resumed her crying.

And crying.

And crying.

And crying some more.

Nothing I did could soothe her.

By this time, many of my friends had come by asking what was wrong. I had no idea. I wished Olive was there – she would know what to do. I started feeling embarrassed. My friends were going to think I was a terrible father and that I didn't spend any time with Allie, which is why I couldn't get her to stop crying.

I tried changing her diaper. Both my sister and brother-in-law tried soothing her. None of it worked.

"What's wrong?" my concerned friends continued to ask.

"I think she's tired," I said, feeling the need to have an explanation but having absolutely no idea what was happening. After what seemed like an eternity more of trying to calm Allie and her still crying, I decided to give up.

I said a quick apologetic goodbye to everyone, wished happy birthday to the birthday girl, packed up, and whisked my crying baby out the door.

As I strapped Allie into her car seat I braced myself for a long drive home. But as I started driving, she stopped crying and fell asleep.

On the way home, I reflected on the experience. I felt embarrassed for not being able to calm my baby down. This was a basic parenting skill. But more than embarrassment, I felt disappointment. I was really looking forward to showing off my baby to my friends. I wanted to share my joy with them and have them be enthralled by my baby's cuteness. All they got was my baby's cries. My disappointment was partly due to the terrible first impression Allie had made, but more so, the terrible first impression I had made as a new dad.

When I got home I told my sob story to Olive, who comforted me.

[Olive]

I've learned that as a parent, whether I like it or not, a part of my ego is tied to how well received our baby is. I wasn't at the party where Allie cried inconsolably, but there have been countless other times where I wanted Allie to impress someone and it just didn't happen.

One time, we were at our friends' home attending their baby dedication service where close friends and family gathered to bless and pray for their newborn son. Allie was a couple months old at the time. I had just spoken and everyone was still looking in our direction. It was a quiet, solemn moment. All of a sudden, Allie let out a loud, long poop. We all laughed, of course. But I was inwardly mortified.

Another time, when Allie was six months old, I walked with her to our local grocery store. It was the middle of summer and a pretty hot day. We picked up a few things and lined up at the checkout. As we stood there waiting, Allie suddenly threw up all over the floor. The elderly couple behind us was wonderfully gracious and helped to clean up her mess. But again, I was terribly embarrassed.

It's especially frustrating when the people I want her to impress are family members – like our parents. Both sets of them live in other cities and we try to foster familiarity with regular Skype calls. But inevitably, the first couple days of their visit, Allie will act cautious around them and cry if they try to come too close to her.

I want to think that with our good parenting skills, we have groomed our child to be charming, polite and responsive to the people we meet. The only problem is she is a baby. And unless these people see her every day, they are pretty much strangers to her. So of course she will cry – or at best, stare them down.

Still, it's hard not to feel embarrassed or disappointed that this little extension of me did not make a good impression. Even though it's completely not her fault. The thing is, how others think of her does not actually reflect my own worth either. That's the silly thing about our egos.

40

Contemplative

Pondering the Beginning and End of Life

[Tim]

My cousin called to let us know that my grandpa had another stroke. The nurses said he probably only had a few days to live – at best. I knew we had to go see him. We packed up Allie and drove to the care home where he was staying. On the way we stopped by McDonald's for a quick bite to eat – my grandpa loved McDonald's and always brought us there when we were growing up.

When we reached the care home, my cousins and aunt greeted us. Everyone was feeling somber and down. I'm glad we brought Allie, because she brought some joy and laughter to everyone. As we sat there in the room, I reflected on how similar Allie and my grandpa were – Allie being a baby at the beginning of her life, and my 91-year-old grandpa who was at the end of his life.

Allie was conceived around the same time my

grandfather had his first major stroke. As Allie grew bigger and stronger, my grandfather grew thinner and weaker. After my grandpa had the stroke, he lost many of his abilities. He could not speak. He would grunt and make noises to try to communicate, much like Allie did. As my father, aunts and uncle took turns bathing my grandpa, feeding him, changing his diaper, and wheeling him around in his wheelchair, Olive and I bathed Allie, fed her, changed her diapers, and wheeled her around in her stroller. My grandpa had to eat puréed foods and later had to be fed from a tube. When Allie was in Olive's belly she gained her nutrition through the umbilical cord (like a tube), then later ate puréed foods. Both Allie and my grandpa slept in short chunks, both day and night.

Seeing their similarities, I was struck by how a person's beginning and end of life are so fragile. To survive, we rely on the people who love us to take care of us.

One day, I will have the honour and privilege of caring for my aging parents like they cared for me as a baby. And one day, Allie will have to care for Olive and me like we cared for her as a baby.

It's the cycle of life. We give and receive. We support and are supported. We love and are loved.

[Olive]

For a brief moment, a baby's laughter filled the room where a frail, 91-year-old man lay dying. The child was my daughter. The man was her great-grandfather. This was the second and final time she would ever meet him in her life.

We gathered around his bedside. Six grandchildren by

blood, two grandchildren by marriage, and one great-grandchild.

Allie, of course, would never remember that moment. Her world consisted only of a limited awareness of those familiar to her, things to play with and food. She wouldn't know the solemness of those hours. Her concern was mostly for when she could get her next corn puff. But her presence there was equally important. Although she was oblivious to our grief, her babbling reminded us to be grateful. Her outstretched hand looking to touch our fingers with hers brought us a measure of hope. Yes, we were losing someone dear, but one look at her told us not all was lost.

So we mourned. We mourned the passing of a once strong and proud man who gave us the legacy of the Chan name. We treasured the memories of conversations over dim sum. We grappled with the hole that was now left in our family. And in the midst of it, we heard a baby's giggle, and we found consolation.

41

Grateful

It Really Does Take a Village

[Olive]

My heart floods with gratitude every time I think of all the people who rallied around us in our first year of parenthood. From the moment we announced the news of our pregnancy, friends and family offered us endless support. Most of my maternity clothing was lent to me, as are most of Allie's clothes. When we set up the nursery, we barely needed to buy any baby items because people were so eager to give us stuff.

One of the best gifts we received in the early months of Allie's life was when a group of our friends from church came over one evening and told us to give them a list of errands for them to do. What they accomplished in a matter of hours would have taken us weeks to finish. One of our friends even deep-cleaned our whole bathroom for us – something that I had been desperate to do but hadn't had the time or energy to tackle.

We also couldn't have managed to move from our apartment to a house without the help of our friends who packed, lifted, loaded and unloaded boxes upon boxes. And they all came with only a few days' notice.

Aside from physical help, there were friends who called or emailed to check up on us. And there were friends who I would call with my frantic first-time-mom questions. There were also online friends, people I'd never even met before, who responded to my "How do I get snot out of my baby's nose?" kind of questions out of the wisdom of their mothering experiences.

Finally, there were the friends who called *us* with their first-time parent questions. They might not have realized they were helping us, but in asking us for our opinions, they enabled us to feel like some of our hard-learned lessons weren't going to waste. It was a gift to be able to pass on some of the love and wisdom we'd received.

Parenthood is like a club and the first year is a pretty intense initiation. Something about having the enormous task of raising a tiny human moves us to reach out to others, to be supported and to support others in return. The first year of parenthood showed me just how valuable and beautiful it is that we get to live in community.

[Tim]

A commonly used phrase in our culture is, "It takes a village to raise a child." I believe it also takes a village to raise first-time parents. There's a lot of growing up that we needed to do as new parents and we couldn't have made it without the support, encouragement, and help of our "village" of friends and family.

Being in community is a beautiful thing. Every person is able to share what he or she has to benefit others, and in turn, receive what others give.

We have received our community's physical gifts. A mere glance at our family room confirms this. Most of the toys that Allie plays with were lent or given to us. Our friends and family have generously given Allie "red pockets," which in Asian culture is a monetary gift traditionally given at holidays or special occasions, allowing us to start a college fund for her.

We have received our community's gifts of time and care. Our friends and family have helped to babysit Allie so Olive and I can take a nap, go out on a rare date or work on this book.

We have received our community's gifts of their strengths, skills, and talents. My mother-in-law is an excellent chef who cooks delicious meals for us. My father-in-law is a wonderful handyman who fixes up our house whenever he is here. Both my parents are trained counselors who ask us insightful questions and listen closely to our responses. My friend who loves extreme couponing always lets us know when there are special discounts on baby products, so we can save money. The list goes on and on.

Most importantly, we have received our community's gift of love, for Olive, myself, and Allie. We know that they will always be there when we need them, and that we are not alone in this journey of parenthood.

George Bernard Shaw says, "I am of the opinion that my life belongs to the whole community and as long as I live, it is my privilege to do for it whatever I can. I want to be thoroughly used up when I die, for the harder I work the more I live." As much as we have been blessed to receive from our community, we are more blessed to be able to give. There is a deep sense of meaning when Olive and I can share what we have, our material possessions, our time, our strengths, our skills, and our love, with those in our community.

It is our hope that Allie will grow up in community, that she can be shaped and influenced by our family and friends who love her. And that she will enrich their lives in return.

Epilogue

Allie's First Birthday

[Tim]

December 6th, 2012 was Allie's first birthday. I could barely believe that it had only been a year. So much had happened. Our daughter had learned and changed so much.

A year ago she was a helpless tiny baby who only knew how to blink and fart. Now at the 1-year mark, Allie could smile and laugh. She could crawl and almost stand on her own. She babbled constantly. She could give out high-fives and wave goodbye. She was learning to communicate her desires by pointing her index finger, display her affection through hugging, and show her discomfort through whining.

Over the course of one year she had become a little person. It was a great joy to experience her growth and her change. Even so, it felt like we were just starting to understand who she was.

Throughout the year I found myself thinking about the deeper questions of life. What is the meaning of life? How do I live my life to the fullest? How do I make my life count?

Being a parent forced me to seriously consider these questions, because it was now my responsibility to help teach my kid what life was all about. It's my desire to teach our child about love, joy, hope, and courage. About living freely and being responsible, about being kind and generous, about working hard and trusting others, about practicing gratitude in the midst of varying circumstances, and about living authentically.

American professor of physics Frank Oppenheimer said, "The best way to learn is to teach."

Perhaps the greatest gift of being a parent is getting the opportunity to teach my child what life is all about, and in the process, learning about it myself.

[Olive]

The day Alena turned one year old we gave ourselves the day off to celebrate. We whipped up some fresh waffles for breakfast to commemorate the occasion. So much had changed since we first held our tiny bundle in that hospital room. Our child had grown so much. We had all grown.

We had survived the first year of parenthood. 365 days as a family of three, and we had lived to tell about it. We felt a profound sense of relief and accomplishment. We had survived meltdowns, sleepless nights, incessant crying, sickness, new skills, and boredom. We had survived new teeth, falls, bruises, explosive poops, no poops and daily new discoveries.

Somehow, knowing that we had lived through our first year as parents made me believe that from now on, we could survive anything that life might throw at us.

In this year, I learned that parenthood is a lot about making room for another person. In a sense, it's one of life's greatest lessons in hospitality.

As Alena's mother, there is a lot that I need to give her – my attention, energy and time, for example. Yet I receive just as much, if not more, from her. She has enlarged my heart with her indiscriminate curiosity toward people. She has plunged me into the throes of grace as I've had to let go of my need to control outcomes and timelines. She has opened my eyes to the wonder and beauty of the world as together we've examined pebbles, played simple games and crunched autumn leaves between our fingers. She has stretched my patience and forced me to face my fears. She has made me laugh more than I ever thought was possible.

The first year of motherhood was an intense course in responsibility, persevering through challenges and embracing all that it means to be human.

Allie was, and continues to be, my subject of study and my teacher.

Notes

1. "Crash Course" Cambridge Dictionaries Online. Web. 7 Mar 2013. <http://dictionary.cambridge.org>

2. Yee, Krystal. "How Much Does it Cost to Raise Kids in Canada?" Canadian Living. Web. 7 Mar 2013. <http://www.canadianliving.com>

3. "Cost of Raising a Child" Baby Center. Web. 7 Mar 2013. <http://www.babycenter.com>

4. Hananel, Sam. "Cost Of Raising A Child Climbs To $235,000 For Middle-Income Families" Huffington Post. 14 Jun 2012. Web. 7 Mar 2013. <http://www.huffingtonpost.com>

5. Matthew 6:34, New International Version. Grand Rapids: Zondervan, 1986.

Acknowledgements

Writing a book is like raising a baby. We simply could not do it alone.

We want to extend special thanks to our family: Ben, Bernadette, Louis, Janice, Dan, Melissa, Tiff, Simon, and Alena for their love, their constructive feedback and for believing in us.

Thank you, Jackie, Lisa, Lucas, and Cam, for being our editors and focusing the direction and message of our book. Thanks also to Sarah, Gideon, Tiff, Pearline, Leo, Josh, and Lisa for doing the fine-comb editing of catching typos and grammatical errors. Any mistakes that remain are solely our fault.

We are grateful, too, for our stellar book launch team: Amanda, Arthur, Belinda, Benjamin, Christopher, Donna, Esther, Gideon, Hubert, Jane, Jess, Jonathan, Leo, Nouver, Paul, Ricky, Sally, and Thomas. Thank you for sharing in this experience.

Thanks to Bill Vaxevanis, who helped us design the book cover and patiently did countless revisions until it was just right. And we're thankful for Donna and Nouver of Wakefield Productions for creating a stellar book trailer.

We are also very appreciative of our blog readers, who have shown us much support and encouragement since our blog launched in 2011.

Thanks to God for giving us the privilege of becoming parents, and for this season of life to write this book.

About the Authors

When no one's around to hear them at home, Tim and Olive's life turns into a musical. Some of their best memories together include eating at a seaside McDonald's in Casablanca, riding bikes around Barcelona, having pasta in Panama to celebrate their first Valentine's Day  together, and making banana-nutella crepes for brunch.

Tim is a cheerful pessimist born in Yellowknife. He holds a business degree and has worked in logistics and non-profit. He loves mangos, snowboarding, mentoring, the Vancouver Canucks, analyzing everything, and laughing with his daughter. His favourite person is his wife. Tim works as a social media, marketing, and blogging consultant.

Olive is an artsy optimist who grew up in Toronto. Her favourite place in the world is her home. A contemplative at heart, she aspires to be a conduit of grace, rest and beauty in this hurried and chaotic world.

Tim and Olive were married in the autumn of 2008 and live with their daughter Alena near Vancouver, Canada. They regularly blog about thoughtful marriage, parenting, and life at www.timandolive.com.

Also by these Authors

Refreshingly engaging and unabashedly honest, *Fight With Me: How We Learned to be Married* is one couple's account of their attempts to start their marriage well.

In this fun, approachable and practical book, Tim and Olive draw from their real-life stories to offer an inside look at the triumphs and failures they encountered as they learned to be husband and wife. Written with both of their perspectives, this little gem is not a "how-to" guide but rather a "how-we" companion for anyone who longs for deeper relationships.

Fight With Me has been downloaded by over 5000 people since it was released in October 2012. The book has made it to Amazon's Top 100 Bestseller List and was #1 on Amazon's Top Marriage Books List.

49898098R00095

Made in the USA
San Bernardino, CA
07 June 2017